WOMEN WHO BRAND

WOMEN
WHO BRAND

HOW SMART WOMEN PROMOTE
THEMSELVES AND GET AHEAD

Catherine Kaputa

nb

NICHOLAS BREALEY
PUBLISHING

BOSTON · LONDON

This revised edition published by Nicholas Brealey Publishing in 2014. First published as *The Female Brand* in 2009.

20 Park Plaza, Suite 610	3–5 Spafield Street, Clerkenwell
Boston, MA 02116, USA	London, EC1R 4QB, UK
Tel: + 617-523-3801	Tel: +44-(0)-207-239-0360
Fax: + 617-523-3708	Fax: +44-(0)-207-239-0370

www.nicholasbrealey.com

Special discounts on bulk quantities of Nicholas Brealey Publishing books are available to corporations, professional associations, and other organizations. For details, contact us at 617-523-3801.

Printed in the United States of America.

20 19 18 17 16 15 14   1 2 3 4 5 6 7 8 9 10

ISBN: 978-1-85788-624-5
E-ISBN: 978-1-85788-998-7

Library of Congress Cataloging-in-Publication Data
Kaputa, Catherine, 1948–
Women who brand : how smart women promote themselves and get ahead / Catherine Kaputa.
pages   cm
Summary: "Just as individual strengths are based on who we are as people, gender-based strengths for women are essential assets of the female brand. Out of this provocative and challenging assertion, Women Who Brand delivers the very latest in gender research into the female brain to debunk the notion that women have to play the male game to win"— Provided by publisher.
ISBN 978-1-85788-624-5 (paperback) — ISBN 978-1-85788-998-7 (e-book)   1. Businesswomen. 2. Success in business. 3. Career development. 4. Women in the professions. 5. Businesswomen—Case studies.   I. Title.
HD6053.K373 2014
650.1082—dc23
2014013360

For my mother,

Carmen Lockwood Kaputa,

and all the women like her,
who have inspired countless millions
since the dawn of time

CONTENTS

INTRODUCTION

It's Time for Women to Brand

Ever since a certain assertive female decided she wanted to eat fruit from a certain forbidden tree, women have been loved, hated, glorified, vilified, and misunderstood. Our modern world, of course, is no different. Today, however, in many ways we are shedding the rigid ideas that were commonplace just a generation ago and venturing into a brave new world of adventure, opportunity, and angst.

Women first entered the workplace in great numbers out of necessity in World War II. The enormity of the war effort meant that millions of men would need to be mobilized for the task. Men couldn't be in two places at once. So if men were busy driving jeeps, who was making the jeeps?

Rosie the Riveter, That's Who

Quaint notions of the weaker sex and a woman's place were swept aside in an instant. Saving the world came first. Victory brought the men back to the factories, but nothing could bring back the world that had been. Changes to come would, for better or worse, remake the family, the workplace, and the world.

To understand the future of the workplace, it's important to realize how relatively new our economic reality is. Well into the twentieth century, women's lives were centered around home and family, as were most men's, since most people still lived on the farm. The so-called Industrial Revolution laid the foundation of our current commercial world. Commerce, of course, has always existed, but it has become an overwhelming presence and has dramatically affected our lives.

In a blink of historical time, we've gone from making our own clothes and growing our own food to making only money. Stereotypes of women have changed dramatically in my lifetime alone. When I was growing up in the 1950s and '60s, women were viewed as not-quite-as-good versions of men. Women of my generation were encouraged to go after "pink" jobs like nursing and teaching. While these are worthwhile pursuits, why should women be limited?

In the '70s, the women's liberation movement threw a torch at thinking pink and claimed that there are no differences between men and women, only stereotypes. We could be and do anything. Women started going after all kinds of jobs and succeeding. Storming the gates of the male workplace, though, came at a cost for women. We had to submerge our families and try to be superwomen.

Science created another sea change that affected the role of women in society. Women's biological role was revolutionized, and women were liberated in attitude, biology, and opportunity.

Opportunity Means the *Chance* to Succeed

Opportunity doesn't mean things are equal or that you *will* succeed. If only it were that simple! Things are not necessarily equal for men, either, though it's women who typically have to go the extra mile. Nevertheless, a major change is taking place today, too, as companies embrace diversity in the workforce.

Today, women are influencing the workplace, and many companies are trying to make it easier for women, with diversity or women's initiatives, flextime, and opt-out programs that accommodate child rearing. Even though the image of women in the workplace has evolved dramatically, we're still not where we want to be. We're still in transition.

The number of women in the workforce continues to increase, mainly because women do a good job—particularly with our modern jobs. As the Western world moves further and further away from basic manufacturing work and as machines replace people, cooperation, verbal skills, organization, and teamwork are more valued. Increasingly, skills and temperaments considered more female than male are what help make one successful in the twenty-first century.

Remarkable new research on gender differences in neuroscience, psychology, and social science questions the original women's liberation notion that men and women are the same. In many ways, the most revealing research, and the hardest to deny, comes from the emerging field of neuroscience because it uses magnetic resonance imaging (MRI) and positron-emission tomography (PET) scans to record what actually takes place in the brains of women and men as they perform different activities. There is also a lively debate about gender issues taking place among evolutionary psychologists, who look at evolution as the basis for the development of gender differences and culture.

The Different Way Women and Men Approach a Task

Many gender differences show up in studies of behavior dynamics. One landmark study involved male and female children—prepubescent children, so that even the influence of hormones is eliminated as much as possible. The study demonstrates some basic differences in approach that are germane to the workplace and society in general. These differences are reflected in what I call a "male brand" and a "female brand." Children were separated into all-boy and all-girl groups and given a task to complete cooperatively. The girls used their social skills and worked together and formed a kind of committee. They all took part in discussions about how to accomplish the task. Meanwhile, the boys jostled around and picked a leader, and then the leader directed the effort to get the job done.

Both in their way had positive outcomes. But each gender used very different models. When the groups were given tasks that were too hard or difficult to accomplish, the boys wound up screaming and fighting among themselves, while the girls became moody and withdrawn.

Yes, there are downsides to gender, too. When things are out of whack, men are more likely to sink into antisocial behaviors like violence, aggression, and alcohol abuse, while women tend to turn inward and experience eating disorders, panic attacks, and depression.

I became intrigued with the larger question: Is there a female brand distinct from the male variety? And what are its advantages in the workplace? Is our biology, in fact, not a weakness that we should try to ignore while hoping for it to disappear?

Of course, in many areas, there aren't significant differences between women and men. But I have become convinced that in other ways there are important differences in aptitude, preference, and motivation that have a big effect on women's approach to their professional and personal lives. Just as we each have individual strengths based on who we are as people, we have gender-based strengths as women that are important assets of the female brand.

Tune In to Your Wiring

Turns out Mom was right. She always said, "Boys will be boys and girls will be girls."

We *are* wired differently. "Not that there's anything wrong with that," to quote Jerry Seinfeld. We don't need a million-dollar research study to tell us that what we are and how we are—how we think and how we behave—are different. Just go to a playground and watch girls and boys play.

I used to think that many gender differences resulted from being raised differently. To say that our biology has some effect on our minds and how we see the world still strikes some as un-American. We shouldn't be determined by anything, right? But once I had a son, I could see with my own eyes how differently the genders are wired from the beginning. How much is due to genes? How much to hormones? Trying to eliminate any taint from the social environment, Professor Simon Baron-Cohen videotaped more than one hundred infants at one day old. His study showed that baby girls were most attracted to a mobile of a face, and baby boys were more fixated on a mechanical mobile.

It's fascinating to watch the toys that each gender likes to play with. By and large, girls are more fascinated with faces and people—by dolls and playing house. Boys are fascinated by things—by cars and construction sets. Both casual observation and academic studies by Baron-Cohen and others confirm these preferences.

So how does this play out in life—girls and people versus boys and things?

One basic difference is women's tendency to be more social and to focus on people and connection. We tend to have good radar for detecting the effect we have on others and sensing their feelings. And that can be a two-edged sword. One study focused on fourth-grade Israeli children running on a track. There was no speed difference between the boys and girls until competition was thrown into the mix. When they were put in paired groups to run, the boys ran faster and the girls ran slower. And the girls ran slowest of all when running with another girl.

In contrast to a woman's interest in empathy and connection, studies by Baron-Cohen and others show that men have a more outward orientation and focus on understanding and building systems. Of course there are exceptions, but on the whole women are a people-oriented brand and men are a thing-oriented brand.

●   ●   ●

The female brain is hardwired for empathy and connection.
The male brain is hardwired for building systems.

✻ ✻ ✻

Hormones rev up our natural instincts toward connection even more. As girls become teens, they focus even more on personal emotions and intimate relationships, because when estrogen floods the brain, it bolsters female social skills with an intense drive toward connection. Estrogen and oxytocin also help power women's intuition and empathy. Motherhood brings about more changes and hormones, driving an overriding urge to nurture, avoid conflict, and build connection with others. With menopause, women experience a final shift in hormones. Estrogen and oxytocin are lower. Now, rather than being driven by a desire to connect with and nurture others, we women, often for the first time, focus on ourselves. At last we give ourselves permission to do our own thing.

Now, the disclaimer. Female qualities are not limited to women. We all have both male and female in us. And it's possible for a man to be more female than a woman. As groups, men are more masculine and women are more feminine, but as individuals, that's not necessarily so. (Just as, in general, men are taller than women, but plenty of women are taller than plenty of men—just ask Michelle Obama or Tom Cruise.) The point is that men can learn from getting in touch with their feminine side as much as women can.

The Remarkable Female Brain

Because some gender studies have displayed contradictory results, one of the hottest areas in gender research is the field of neuroscience, which studies the structure and function of the brain and nervous system. While the male and female brains are similar in so many ways, neuroscientific studies point to some female advantages and aptitudes: strong empathetic ability, verbal skills, keen emotional responsiveness, and other advantages

To make their discoveries, neuroscientists use a four-ton device called a functional magnetic resonance imaging (fMRI) scanner. These machines record changes in the oxygen level of blood feeding the brain. Because the brain rapidly supplies blood to working areas, active areas virtually light up to provide a mini-movie of what's going on. A "brain-to-brain dance" takes place when we connect with another person, and different areas of the brain "light up" during certain activities in men and in women.

One interesting difference shown in the MRI pictures is that most women use both the right and left hemispheres of the brain for processing verbal, visual, and emotional experiences. Men use only one. The bundle of nerves connecting the two hemispheres is also thicker in women, making for a wide boulevard of connection. And that's not the end of it. A neuroscientist counted the neurons in the brain tissue of men and women—thin slice by thin slice—and found that the female brain is densely packed with 11 percent more neurons in the language area.

Women Are Just as Smart as Men

Most women are smaller than men, and the female brain is about 9 percent smaller. This size advantage led some scientists to speculate that men were smarter than women. But it turns out that women have just as many brain cells as men. Our brain cells are just packed more tightly into a smaller braincase.

Women are just as smart as men, too, if you look at average intelligence. But men are smarter in the way they talk about their intelligence. Men tend to overestimate their intelligence, and women tend to underestimate their smarts.

✻   ✻   ✻

The average IQ of women and men is about even,
though men tend to overestimate *and*
women tend to underestimate *their intelligence.*

✻   ✻   ✻

This tendency to play dumb about our intellectual capabilities is something we must resist. The most obvious reason that you don't want to downplay your intelligence is that people may believe you! But there is a more subtle, and perhaps even more profound reason you don't want to disparage your intelligence. You might start to believe it! Success is determined not just by how smart you are, but by how smart you *feel* in comparison to others. When you feel smart, you're confident and that will make it easier to shine in any setting. Likewise, when you don't feel smart, you won't project the confidence and gravitas that's needed in important situations.

Preferences and Prejudices

Memories of old-fashioned thinking about female intellectual ability added fuel to the fire that engulfed Lawrence Summers, the former president of Harvard University. Summers made a remark in a speech questioning whether the relative scarcity of women in science was due to innate differences in ability between men and women. The story took on a life of its own in the media, and Summers's comments generated such a storm of protest that he thought it best to resign.

It's true that there are fewer women working in the sciences and math, but it's not lack of ability that is holding us back. Tests show that women can do math and science extremely well.

Perhaps science and math aren't presented in the right way for women, and these fields have a male brand-image (the computer nerd) that discourages women, similar to the guys-only image of top corporate jobs.

The real reason may be the simplest and most profound. Many women aren't interested in math and science as careers. Women often think of math and science as too abstract and systems oriented (a male preference) and not sufficiently people and content oriented (a female preference). One study showed that people who liked to work with tools or machines were more likely to choose information technology careers. People who liked working with people were a lot less likely to choose IT careers (more women fall into this camp).

One landmark study followed more than three thousand mathematically precocious boys and girls from middle school to middle age over a thirty-five-year period. All were gifted in math, but when it came time to choose a career, a chasm emerged. The men selected engineering and physical sciences, and the women were more likely to choose medicine, biological sciences, humanities, and the social sciences.

In short, this large-scale study over three decades showed that mathematically strong men prefer to work with "inorganic" things in fields involving machines, abstractions, and the like. The women, in general, prefer to work with "organic" or living things in fields involving social interaction with people and helping people.

Something else in this study was startling. The women had more options. Women who were gifted in math were more likely than the men to have strong verbal skills, too. So they could choose careers in science or become lawyers, marketers, or teachers. The males who were good in math tended to have weak verbal skills.

Do you see what is so fascinating? Women can excel at both math/science and the liberal arts while it is unusual for men to be outstanding in both arenas. Many men with the deepest math and science skills tend to be one-trick ponies and can't compete in nontechnical areas. This has been common enough to have become a major cliché, "computer nerd."

The Freedom to Choose

In school you have a choice between getting a broad education in the liberal arts that makes you a more well-rounded person and getting a specialized education that's more marketable in terms of a job. I would never advise people not to go with their passion, but you should keep in mind that if your passion is in an obscure or low-demand area, then you are going to struggle or else have to get very good at branding yourself.

Although a broad liberal arts education is valuable, you will find that for landing that first job, it's generally more beneficial to major in something practical like finance, marketing, accounting, engineering, computer science, or physics and study your passion on the side. You'll graduate with more marketable credentials.

Let's look at the gender gap in the sciences. The gender divide in the sciences is greatest in countries that allow women the most freedom to choose. For example, there are five to seven times more females in the hard sciences (such as physics) in Russia and the Philippines than in Canada, the United Kingdom, or the United States. And most of the girls who succeed in math in the U.S. are immigrants or the daughters of immigrants.

As barriers come down, gender gaps seem to widen. With more opportunities, we have choices. For most women, a career in technology or the hard sciences doesn't match our DNA. We're in a culture where math and IT have a decidedly male, nerdy brand image. It doesn't fit our brand unless it's a people-oriented job like medicine or a people-oriented role like sales and marketing in a technology or science company. And it's doable. About 70 percent of the jobs in IT companies are nonprogramming jobs and are highly "organic," involving strong interpersonal skills.

If, like many women, we're good at both, we may like math but love literature and the humanities. This is freedom.

Creating a Brand That's in Demand

But are women smart in avoiding technical credentials in today's marketplace, particularly if they're good at math? A key goal of personal branding is to create a brand that's in demand. Today, graduates with a liberal arts degree have a difficult time finding jobs while graduates with STEM degrees are gobbled up quickly, often receiving multiple offers. As one media theorist said, "Code is literacy in the twenty-first century."

Many women choose marketing as a college major, but marketing and advertising are being transformed by the digital onslaught just like every other industry. Ad agencies used to be roughly equal in terms of a female/male split, but now agencies tend to skew male due to the impact of social media and digital marketing where programming and data analytics are critical. So if you are choosing a marketing career, it would be wise to pick up some programming, data analytics, and digital media courses along the way.

Maybe we need to rebrand technical careers by launching a television series that takes place at a fast-paced technology company or digital marketing agency so that women can see just how dynamic and varied digital-related careers can be. It's not just about coding in front of a computer screen all day. There are salespeople, marketers, customer care people and many other functions. Plus many women might discover they have a flair for coding and technological innovation.

Tap Into the Female Leadership Style

Of course, each of us develops her own personal leadership style, but there are characteristics of the female brand that many of us instinctually gravitate toward. We tend to have a big-picture orientation. Women leaders are more like mentors or coaches, favoring collaboration, involving colleagues in making decisions, and nurturing the various members of the team. We tend to be highly intuitive and more people oriented in making leadership decisions and more service oriented in dealing with clients. We can be great talent developers, and at the end of the day, the quality of the people can

xviii WOMEN WHO BRAND

make the difference between a company that does just okay and one that clicks.

Again, it's a generalization, but the male brand tends to be more of a command-and-control type. Men are often more objective and analytical in making leadership decisions. The male style is powerful, too, with its focus on analysis and getting the system to work in the best way.

What you want to do is to lead with a style that's natural to you, and don't try to be like a man if that's not your style. Otherwise, we won't use what's different and powerful about our exceptional advantages and style, our singular abilities and sensibilities, which can give the female brand an edge in the workplace and everyplace.

Leverage Your Female Edge

Branding is about leveraging your edge over competitive brands. The female mindset gives us powerful aptitudes that we should leverage in the workplace for career success:

- **Exceptional empathy.** We've got antennae that are terrific at reading gestures, tone of voice, faces, and postures. In short, we can read between the lines and know what's really going on with someone.

- **Uncanny intuition.** We can go with our gut. We often know the answer through an unconscious process that can be remarkably accurate and insightful.

- **Strong verbal and communication skills.** Women score better in reading comprehension, writing, and other verbal skills, all of which are crucial in the workplace.

- **The social gene and the ability to build deep personal relationships.** Women are better at connecting with and nurturing other people. Women specialize in building strong, supportive relationships.

- **More openness in communicating and sharing feelings.** Women are more willing to open up, start talking, and share their emotions. We are more likely to speak out about problems that are affecting morale in the workplace.

- **Collaborative, team-oriented leadership style.** Rather than turning to a command-and-control leadership style, women tend to build consensus and lead with active group participation.

- **More appearance tools at our disposal.** Women can use their flair and sense of style to create a stronger visual identity through clothing, hairstyles, makeup, and accessories—a core component of personal branding.

Work the Female-Brand Advantage

Look at the aptitudes of males and females listed below. Of course, none is carved in stone for any individual, but they represent tendencies and orientations wired into most of us because of our gender. As women, we have strong proficiencies based on our verbal prowess, our keen abilities to read the room and connect with people, and our collaborative and community-building skills. These characteristics are essential to brand building. Even our variety and range of personal style and wardrobe give us an advantage in building a strong visual identity. It's a brand manager's dream.

MALE MINDSET	FEMALE MINDSET
Commander	Team leader
Individuality	Connection
Competition	Collaboration
Narrower focus	Big picture
Facts and figures	Story and context
Reason	Intuition
Employees	Community
Analysis	Empathy
More and shallower relationships	Fewer and deeper relationships
Large groups	Small groups
More homogenous appearance	More differentiated appearance
Thinker	Feeler
Things and systems	People
Spatial ability	Language ability

A More Balanced Approach

Gender expert Roy Baumeister points out that men go to extremes more than women do. He says that we can see this male-female dichotomy in intelligence, in height, in on-the-job risk taking, in status, and in society.

Look at intelligence, which, as we pointed out, is about equal. Men are more often at the extremes here, too. There are more men at the top of the IQ heap and also more men at the bottom. There are fewer women at the extremes and more in the middle range in intelligence. But overall, average intelligence is about equal.

Look at the business, social, or political pecking order. Men are running most things—at the very top, running large companies and leading nations—but there are more men at the other extreme, too. There are more men by far at the very bottom of society, locked up in our prisons. (Women made up 7 percent of the prison population in 2006.)

Men typically are viewed as the stronger sex, but they are also the weaker sex. Fewer boys than girls survive through birth. Men are more likely by far to have developmental and learning disorders like attention deficit disorder. As adults, men on average have more illnesses and die younger than women (an average life span of seventy-eight years for men versus eighty-four years for women).

Women Who Brand

In my personal branding talks, coaching, and interviews with women, I started exploring how successful women take advantage of their female mindset and assets along with their personal strengths and skills. A core idea of personal branding is that the better you understand yourself, both strengths and weaknesses, the easier it will be to maximize your strong points and compensate for the weak points.

As I thought about *Women Who Brand*, I considered my twenty-plus years working in a wide variety of organizations and all the challenges and people I've met along the way. I certainly did my fair share of moving around, from the cultural world of art museums to the advertising world of Madison Avenue, from marketing financial products on Wall Street to teaching branding in the halls of academe. I've experienced the entrepreneurial highs and lows of running my own personal-brand strategy business. And I began reminiscing about the experiences and the people, particularly the successful women I'd met along the way.

In one of my flashbacks, I was transported back to my first days at the ad agency Wells, Rich, Greene, with its female CEO, Mary Wells Lawrence. The offices at Wells, Rich, Greene were not like the rest of Madison Avenue, just as a sturdy oxford is not like a dainty pump. It was feminine. As soon as you entered the lobby, you felt the warmth and richness of an elegant Park Avenue manse, with vibrant wall treatments, carefully chosen colors and textures, and tasteful art and antiques. This was not your typical corporate office.

A grand staircase was the focal point of the agency. It would be easy to imagine Vivien Leigh or Loretta Young sweeping down elegantly with her skirt gently swaying as she descended. The staircase, naturally, led to Mary's suite of offices. We would meet with clients in the Jade Room or the Duck Room, which I usually chose because its collection of antique duck decoys showed that femininity is complex and not limited to frills, lace, and the color pink.

All the ad execs' offices were fitted out with antique or sleek modern furniture, and what you chose mattered to Mary. A very senior female executive made the mistake of selecting without the proper gravity. When Mary came by and saw her simple Parsons table and bare walls, the next visitor was a moving crew replacing the entire contents of the room. Afterward, this executive had a darling French Provincial desk, striking paisley drapes, and trendy Andy Warhol sketches of flowers on the wall.

Mary Wells Lawrence's unabashedly feminine style as a leader permeated the agency, from the stylish look of the offices, to the personal leadership style she fostered and the way client relationships were nurtured, to the panache of the creative work and our drive to go the extra mile and do our best.

Here was a woman who not only created brands through innovative advertising, she created her own brand. Being a woman who brands was part of her edge.

It's a Women's Dilemma

In the realm of tasks—projects, reports, getting it done—women do a great job. But that is not what counts at the manager level and above. Then it's about getting your ideas heard, motivating a reluctant group, and spearheading projects. What also matters at the manager level is getting your work in front of the right people, building relationships with key executives, and being a good ambassador for Brand You.

The problem for many women is that we don't realize what's needed to project real authority to get ahead. It takes a whole new skill set, primarily soft skills and personal branding skills. With all our verbal agility, we can be reluctant to push our ideas forward forcefully. We don't raise our hands and pitch ourselves for a promotion, a stretch assignment, or a raise. We're too modest and downplay our capabilities. We think self-promotion isn't "nice." We don't know to create positive perceptions about ourselves in the workplace in a way that's authentic and effective. We have trouble building a personal brand or finding the right career and a fulfilling life.

Many of us are insecure about our power, particularly if we work in a male-dominated company (and most of us do). Some women are too timid and reluctant to assert themselves. And who can criticize them? It can be different for women in the business world. If you come on too strong and appear aggressive like men do all the time, you can be disliked. It's hard to get your behavior pitch perfect with the right amount of assertiveness and the right amount of femininity.

How Do You Cope?

Whether we supported her or not, many of us felt Hillary Clinton's pain when she ran for president of the United States in 2008. Or we cringed in sympathy or embarrassment for Sarah Palin when she ran for vice president that same year. Both women had to struggle with how their image was coming across in the media and with voters.

We could identify with the challenges Clinton and Palin faced as female candidates trying to get into the boys' club. Many of us have faced similar difficulties in the professional world, especially if we're ambitious and interested in doing more, or if we've tried to break new ground in a role that was previously male-only turf. From a marketing perspective, we're female brands trying to get shelf space in a market dominated and controlled by male brands.

It's one thing for Clinton and Palin to be critiqued on their politics and points of view, but their hair and clothing were also critiqued. Nothing was off limits, not even Sarah's shoes or the thickness of Hillary's ankles. In debates with male opponents, each woman's voice, pitch, and tone were scrutinized, not just the content of their answers.

Laughing too loud or coming close to tears in front of a reporter was a big media story for Hillary—even her authenticity was called into question after she choked up when asked how she copes each day. And then to top it all off, there was CBS reporter Katie Couric's interview of Sarah Palin that was famously channeled by Tina Fey on *Saturday Night Live*. In one swoop, Palin got branded as a ditz, Couric's hard-news credentials were refurbished, and Fey's star power shot into the stratosphere.

Gender Can Be a Sensitive Issue

Some women, because of past stereotyping, may be skittish about even exploring gender differences. They don't want to be pegged again with "biology is destiny" or turn back feminism's accomplishments.

And who can blame them? My goal is certainly not to continue unfair stereotypes but to provide new insights into the uniqueness of the female mindset and how women can maximize career and life success by using *all* their assets. That means building on your personal strengths, intelligence, and talent, but it also means leveraging your native strengths, instincts, and preferences as a woman: empathy, verbal agility, people orientation, a collaborative leadership style, and visual identity, among other assets. It means thinking in a new way, because the standard brand in business is the male brand. In short, it means thinking and acting to develop your own female brand.

Using all of your assets also means understanding the perceptions in the workplace about women (and yourself individually) so that you can override them or know how far you can push things. After all, none of us works in a vacuum. We work with men and women who often have strong perceptions (right or wrong) about the female brand that are different from perceptions about the male brand. To deny that these perceptions exist is to invite failure. To understand these perceptions gives us power, for then we can disarm them or use them to our advantage.

A How-To and How-To-Think Book

Women Who Brand is about what happens when women take charge of their personal brands instead of leaving career and business success to chance. It's about what happens when women start thinking and acting more creatively and strategically about themselves and their abilities.

The key thing we women need to do is master the art of personal branding. What's holding women back from career success is that we don't brand ourselves as well as men do. We're too modest. We downplay our accomplishments and abilities. We don't think of career options strategically and build a network and personal marketing action plan to get where we want to go. We wait to be tapped rather than pitch ourselves. We don't project confidence and gravitas as much as we'd like. We feel stuck or out of place in a male-dominated workplace.

* * *

Personal branding is how we market the unique value we bring to a professional situation.

* * *

But much of what we consider valuable in our lives comes from conquering difficulties and personal limitations. The act of facing how we're holding ourselves back rather than blaming others produces greatness and beauty.

Women Who Brand is a how-to and how-to-think book for women of all ages who want to create more success, fulfillment, or options. Originally published in hardcover as *The Female Brand*, the book's title has been changed to *Women Who Brand* for the paperback edition, and we've added over 25 percent new content: new stories, new research, new tools.

Successful women are good branders whether they brand themselves consciously or intuitively or whether they admit to it or not. This book will show you how to take back your power and use it. Each chapter contains actionable tips, principles, and tools you can use in branding yourself and getting ahead. You'll learn the essential building blocks for branding yourself for success as well as research about women's aptitudes and preferences and how to leverage the female mindset in business. After all, you don't want to just read about theories or the success of others, you want to learn how to create your own edge.

Interspersed throughout are stories and advice from other professional women—of different ages, in different professions, with different experiences—who faced challenges or opportunities and were forced to respond. Should I play by the rules or trust my own instincts? Shall I go for a risky new assignment or stay put? Shall I consciously network or concentrate on strengthening a few important relationships?

A Female Bard

One of our great reservoirs of wisdom is made up of memorable quotes—small sayings that have endured with countless repetitions because they tell us something about the human experience and about ourselves. I wanted inspiring quotes for this book, and, as I got into the project, all of a sudden I realized I knew a woman whose words were more influential to me, in a way, than even Shakespeare's. Mom. My mother is priceless. And many of the women I interviewed also cited their mothers as the person they most admire. So this book is peppered throughout with quotable wisdom from that other great bard, my mom.

I've often said to my brother and sisters that if our mother had been born later, she would be a CEO running a global company; that's how good she was at running things. She stayed home when we were young, sewed all our clothes, cleaned the house, cooked our meals, and made sure we all did our homework and got good grades. She was the CEO of the family.

I wouldn't be the woman I am today without her as my mom. Mom always told me that I could be anyone I wanted to be and do anything I wanted to do, and that was at a time when girls were encouraged to become teachers if they were smart. She framed my artwork, but the best thing she framed was me.

It's the Best of Times for Women

We're all familiar with the numbers: in the United States and elsewhere in the world, women are well represented at the lower levels and mid levels of organizations, but woefully underrepresented at the more senior levels. Over forty years after the feminist revolution rocked the country, less than 5 percent of Fortune 500 CEOs are women and less than 20 percent of company officers are women at Fortune 500 companies.

Yet I would argue that this is the best of times for women. Career-minded women are leading the charge, inspired by female leaders like Sheryl Sandberg and others. Many companies in every industry are eager to expand the number of women in the upper ranks and are funding women's initiatives and leadership development programs to do just that. Many are under pressure to have more women represented on corporate boards and lament the difficulty in finding qualified women. European countries like Finland and France are mandating that a fixed percentage of corporate board seats go to women, and other countries are discussing following suit.

Some studies show that companies with a healthy percentage of women at senior levels and in the corporate boardroom have better business results, with increased productivity and revenues. In the World Economic Forum's 2013 *Global Gender Gap Report*, countries with the strongest economics are ones that have programs to further women's careers, close the gender pay gap, and keep women—who tend to be better educated than men in most countries—in the workforce after they become mothers. And as we get more women in management roles, I think we'll see more advantages to having gender diversity in our companies and institutions.

So the sands are shifting in our favor. Now, it can be an advantage to be a woman in business. Being a talented woman can open doors and create opportunities, giving you visibility and making possible what might have seemed unthinkable a few years back.

The fact that it's an advantage to be a woman today is important to recognize. For some reason, it is a very difficult lesson for women to learn because being a woman has been a disadvantage in the past in most organizations. Often, women didn't feel they fit in at the boys' club so it was easy to quit trying to advance. Or women made assumptions about what a senior management role would be like and opted to stay in their comfort zone. I'd argue that it's easier and more fulfilling in many ways the higher you go since you have more resources, better compensation, and more power to create culture and make a difference at your organization.

Hard Work + Branding = Success

Thinking like a brand is integral to my approach to career success; it reflects my background in branding and advertising and my work in personal branding. Applying principles and tactics from the commercial world of brands is a smart way to create more success in your life. Branding enables you to think of yourself as a "product" in a competitive marketplace and to differentiate yourself from competitors. It enables you to think outside-in, that is, thinking first of what the market wants and then strategically positioning yourself to meet those needs. Branding forces you to think strategically and creatively as you build an authentic and powerful visual and verbal identity. And no brand would be effective without up-to-date tactics for forging ahead in tough circumstances.

Of course, there is no silver bullet that guarantees you'll reach your dreams, not even having a wise mom as a mentor. If only there were. We'd all love to know the precise series of steps to take—the hurdles we need to jump, the exact list of items we need to check off—that will guarantee our success. There are many things we can do to enhance our chances of success, but, except for two famous things we would all rather avoid, there are no sure things in life.

But some things are clearly necessary if you want to be a successful woman today. Whether you are an executive, a professional, an entrepreneur, a consultant, a coach, an artist, a boomer running a nonprofit in your retirement, or a mom with a website and something to sell, you must craft an identity that's true to you and right for the marketplace— a distinct personal brand—and you must create positive perceptions about yourself in the marketplace.

Women Who Brand is a how-to and how-to-think book for women of all ages who want to create more success, fulfillment, or options. It will show you how to build a strong personal brand in person and online that's authentic, different, and relevant. After all, in today's world, if you don't brand yourself, you will be left behind.

Women Who Brand will provide new insights into why it's different for women in the workplace, how to tap into the aptitudes we're wired for as women, and why playing our game the way men play their game usually backfires. We need to lead with our XX chromosomes!

This book is a high-octane guide for women who want to avoid getting stuck and who want to build a powerful self-brand, network, and confidence—a guide to thriving in today's male-dominated but soon-to-be-female-dominated workplace.

After all, men don't leave their gender-based advantages at the door when they go to work. Neither should women.

Women who brand have
a "different" formula for success:
hard work + branding = success.

1

THE ART OF AUTHENTIC PERSONAL BRANDING

Do you know this woman? She could be working in your office. She could be your college roommate. Or she could be living in your body. She's someone who feels she needs to make a change. She doesn't lack talent or a work ethic, but her life and career don't seem to be on the right track. And she's afraid the train might derail completely. Or maybe she'll just get off the train and walk home.

She knows her workplace has modern attitudes. But something is still wrong. She's unsure of herself. She's not living up to her potential. She's trying to "lean in" and advocate for herself but she's not sure how to do it without being too aggressive.

She's suffering from a problem that affects only women: Female Behavior Confusion Disorder (FBCD).

Too Hot? Too Cold?

What's a woman to do? How do you get it right in the workplace?

Your instincts tell you to "be nice," but if you're too nice you are viewed as weak and not taken seriously. If you are too assertive and exhibit the same leadership qualities that are praised in a man, you risk being called that familiar epithet referring to a female dog that, curiously, has no male equivalent.

It's the Goldilocks dilemma. If you're too hot, you're branded as aggressive or even out of control. If you're too cold, you're labeled an ice queen. The same behavior that's acceptable or admired in a man is often criticized in a woman. It's hard to get it just right.

Even Catalyst, the research organization that's been studying women's leadership and the workplace for more than fifty years isn't sure. But it is sure that a key reason we don't see more women at the higher levels in business is not because of a talent gap but because a self-promotion gap.

The Male Hubris Effect versus the Female Humility Effect

We women have some catching up to do. We're not as good at personal branding as men are. Why is that?

One example of this disparity can be found in the personal columns. The men all sound like Brad Pitt, except even better looking and more accomplished. And what about the women? Well, the women like long walks in the country. (Not exactly the hard sell.) Ladies, that's branding for staying single. If you ask those Brad Pitts what they are looking for in a woman, this long walk thing is not very high on the list. In fact, it's not even on the list.

One male social scientist who did a major global study of male and female business leadership found men are so good at promoting their abilities, they often—believe it or not—exaggerate their abilities and their I.Q., what he branded "The Male Hubris Effect."

Women, on the other hand, tend to lowball their abilities and I.Q., what he dubbed "The Female Humility Effect." The Hubris/Humility Effect shows up in different industries and in different countries. Women judge their abilities worse than they actually are and men judge their abilities as better than they are.

Humility's a Virtue, but Self-Promotion Pays

"Gena" is an ambitious, hardworking executive. In the morning she would often go into work very early and sometimes the CEO would pop in the elevator with her.

Gena was scared to talk. But she was also scared not to talk. So she would talk about the weather.

As she was introduced to the concept of personal branding, Gena started paying more attention to business dynamics and her performance. Then, lo and behold, she found herself in the dreaded elevator with the CEO again. This time a male colleague, Bob, walked in, turned to the CEO, and jauntily said, "John, great to run into you. I'm Bob Smith from sales on the ABC product team. You'll be glad to know that we had a great meeting with a new client this week and we just sealed the deal."

The beaming CEO said, "Bob, you just made my day." And the CEO didn't stop with the proverbial pat on the back, he actually patted Bob on the back as he was getting out of the elevator.

Now, Gena was already learning about personal branding strategies, but there's nothing like a little reality show to convince people to take action. Gena felt like she had been slapped in the face with a fish. Later, in my office, she became reflective.

"Catherine, I saw firsthand what you're talking about. Bob is branding himself as the next VP, and what am I doing? I'm branding myself as the weather girl."

Bingo. Not knowing how to brand ourselves—it's a woman's dilemma. Business has its unspoken rules and procedures that men seem to know well. Winning is the objective, and to win men leverage typically male aptitudes like assertiveness, personal promotion, and confidence. Indeed, these are the signs of leadership.

As Gena told me, her messages growing up were to get along rather than compete, work hard and your work will be rewarded, and don't try to get noticed. Gena got on the personal branding bandwagon and eventually she was recommended by the CEO as a high-potential employee and put on the fast track.

Later, Gena was chosen to run a large division in the Midwest. She told me that becoming a woman who brands was the single most important reason for her success. She overcame her fear of talking to the CEO and other key executives and learned how to authentically promote herself. As she got to know John, the CEO, she discovered that he hated getting into the elevator with employees, because almost everyone froze the minute he stepped in!

Judge a Book by Its Cover

As it did with Gena, branding can make the difference between success and mediocrity. If you don't think branding is important, look at this example from the commercial world: a diet book first published more than fifteen years ago was called *The Modified Carbohydrate Diet*.

Did you ever hear of this diet? Probably not. That sizzling title was created by a Miami doctor. Of course, we're always told, "Don't judge a book by its cover," but we do it every day. Unbranded, the Miami doctor's book didn't do well, selling only a few thousand copies. But so many clients loved the diet that it was passed along through word of mouth.

Then it was branded.

Enter *The South Beach Diet*.

Now the diet had a brand identity that had sizzle. The new name conjured up an image of beautiful people, exciting lifestyles, and the newest happening place. Here was something we like and something we'd like to be part of. The book's cover featured palm trees and Art Deco colors like those found in South Beach. It had a different look— other diet books at the time looked like textbooks. The new brand appealed to people's perceptions. If you like South Beach, you might like the South Beach diet. Nobody really likes modified carbohydrates.

The book got a free celebrity endorsement when a reporter asked then-President Bill Clinton how he lost weight, and he said he went on the South Beach Diet. (Isn't that just like him?) *The South Beach Diet* was one of the first books to capitalize on Internet forums to create an online community of dieters who could further promote the book. So here it is. Smart branding and marketing made this modified carbohydrate diet book a colossal success. These same principles can be key in accomplishing your personal branding.

Hard Power versus Soft Power

Today, for companies and for people, what matters is not "hard power" but "soft power," or branding power, the intangible assets that means so much. It's the soft things that attract people to your brand.

For people, "hard power" is the tangible things you can put on your résumé like years of experience, job history, skills, education, and the like. Hard assets are important but are not enough to compete successfully in today's ultracompetitive environment. We all know lots of people with hard power assets who are underemployed or even unemployed.

For people, soft power, or branding power, is your image and reputation, your network and alliances, your visibility, your communications ability, and the ideas and intellectual property associated with you. Soft power is your emotional connection with your "customers," and we've all got customers. (Your "customers" may be your boss, other executives, and colleagues—a customer is anyone who can affect your brand.)

Soft power is the belief system people have about you. It's standing for something that is valuable in the marketplace. It's having a game plan for success. The fact is, like it or not, branding rules!

So, what is branding, really?

Attach an Idea to Yourself

At its core, branding is about attaching an idea to a product, or an idea to yourself.

You need to attach an idea that's *authentic*, that's based on who you are and your unique strengths and preferences. When you copy, you'll always be second rate.

You also want to find a *different* idea for your brand. Brand managers spend a lot of time delineating differences: a different benefit, different look, different target audience, different process or materials, a different something. In a school of gold fish, you want to be a silver fish.

Your personal brand idea also has to be *relevant*. It has to be something that people value in the arena where you work. For example, my brand idea is that I am a personal brand strategist, not a career or business coach, as many others position themselves. A brand strategist is someone who applies the principles and strategies from the commercial world of brands to your most important product—Brand You.

Becoming a Woman Who Brands

Let's look at personal branding in action. "Liz" had worked at a global company for ten years. She had a large staff but had not been promoted like some other colleagues. Liz had the staff and responsibilities but not the title and compensation. She felt stuck, a common situation for women. Her goal was to have a leadership role and be an officer of the company.

So what was Liz's game plan to achieve her goal?

When I met with Liz, she was upset with her boss, understandably, since she had just been passed over for a promotion yet again. She was so frustrated that she communicated mainly by memo and e-mail. In staff meetings, she sat far from her boss. She let emotions rule.

Let's analyze this. What reaction did Liz want to get from her boss? Liz's goal was to get promoted, to get a better title and more money. Yet, what was she doing to get that reaction? She was avoiding her boss. Is that a good strategy for achieving her goal?"

Don't Let Emotions Trump Strategy

Reacting emotionally in business is a mistake women tend to make. I, too, have often had to fight the "I'm outta here" reaction when I feel someone has done me wrong in business. But reacting emotionally and taking flight are mistakes that women are hardwired to make more often. In my years on Wall Street, I'd see men have a big fight and be best buddies again the next day. Early in my career I was guilty of the opposite, vowing not to speak to the people I was mad at for the rest of my life. Which is the better way to react, from a career perspective?

In my coaching with Liz, I inquired, "What did your boss say when you pitched yourself for a promotion and outlined all your accomplishments over the last two years?"

Liz looked at me in stunned silence. "I didn't ask him," she said. "I didn't pitch myself. He should know what I've done with my team over the last two years. It's been awesome."

This is another dilemma peculiar to women. Women don't ask.

The Power of a Third-Party Endorsement

As I got to know Liz, she told me about an internal position she had applied for the previous year. She had great interviews with a committee of five executives, and Liz felt her credentials were perfect for the role. Liz was upset when she didn't get the position. Later, she found out that the winning candidate, James, hadn't just interviewed with the committee, he reached out to other executives and asked them to advocate for him with committee members they knew. And all these "sponsors," or what we call third-party endorsements or testimonials, turned the contest in James's favor.

So I said to Liz, "Do you know people who you could have called to endorse you?" "Only a few," she admitted. Then Liz said something interesting, "I don't think it's fair. It should just be about your experience, not how good a networker you are."

Of course it's fair; that's the way the business world works.

✹   ✹   ✹

If you say it, it's bragging.
If others say it, it's an expert opinion.

✹   ✹   ✹

Third-party endorsements from satisfied customers, experts, or well-known people are powerful in the branding world because they work. Let other people brag for you, too.

It's Not School Rules Anymore

An important thing for women to realize is that the business world doesn't operate on "School Rules." School rewards studying, completing assignments, and not being disruptive. There is more transparency and reward for industriousness and the only-answer-when-you're-called-on good girl grind.

The business world operates under more fluid rules, under which personal promotion, assertiveness, and getting your work in front of the right people are critical to success. The very traits that make women great students often work against them in the business world. We're waiting to be recognized for all our good work rather than promoting our abilities and pitching ourselves for plum assignments.

So while women outperform men in colleges and graduate schools in terms of GPA and graduation rates, they start to fall behind almost from the moment they enter the workforce. Men are eight times as likely to negotiate their first salary. By the time women reach the mid level in their companies, they feel stuck, and frustration sets in.

What Got You Here, Won't Get You There

Your intelligence and industriousness will get you to the mid level, but you need a whole different set of skills—personal branding skills—if you want to be promoted and perceived as a leader. An important thing to realize is that if you don't take charge of your personal brand, other people will. And they're not likely to brand you in the way you want to be branded.

As smart and hardworking as Liz was, she was holding herself back in ways both large and small by not branding herself. For starters, Liz needed to own her value and be able to pitch herself for a promotion in an elevator speech. We did a "brand audit," looking at Liz's strengths and weaknesses. She was a leader who nurtured her team and led them well in executing projects. So the brand idea we had for positioning Liz was "the empowering leader who gets results," to emphasize that she was a strong leader who people liked working for and who was able to execute large projects successfully.

Her boss, Liz confided, had once told her offhandedly that she "lacked visibility in the company." She was the invisible leader: very task oriented, mainly in her office, not out and about that much.

In branding, visibility is important. That's why brands spend millions of dollars on advertising and PR. There is a visibility premium: if something is visible and well known, we think it is better than something that is invisible and unknown. It must be good, or it wouldn't be so famous, is how the thinking goes.

In business, visibility has a halo effect too. If you're more well known throughout the company, people will assume you're better than someone who is not known. Women can be visibility challenged, focusing on work and not doing the networking and promoting their visibility the way guys do. Liz's boss could even have suggested her for a promotion, and other senior executives may have said, "Liz who?" The assumption often is, if she is so good, I would have heard of her.

Liz also had to start managing up and sideways, building relationships not only with her boss but with other key executives and colleagues, not just managing her team. The upward people are the ones who decide. Having a team who loves you is not enough. Your boss, other executives, and colleagues are important customers for Brand You.

Plus, Liz needed to promote herself and her accomplishments. After all, if no one knows you and your accomplishments, they don't count. It's your job to make them known, not your boss's or other people's jobs to discover them.

All the World's a Meeting

In the business world, the conference room is the stage for Brand You. If you're weak in meetings, you won't appear to be right for the management brand. Liz tended to speak mainly when asked a question at meetings. Her presentations contained lots of detailed bullet points recited in a monotone. When you perform poorly in meetings, you don't appear confident or, even worse, people might think you're lacking in ideas.

Turns out that Liz had an inner critic (The Voice) that second-guessed her and undermined her confidence. It was an inner voice that said, "Be careful what you say, it might be a dumb idea." The inner critic can be a problem particularly with high-achieving women. Fear is what feeds the inner critic: fear of not being good enough, fear of overreaching, fear of not being liked. I've had to fight The Voice, too, and replace negative messages with positive self-talk so that I could be myself and participate fully in business conversations.

Rebranding Takes Action

The number-one market for Liz to target was her boss. Rather than avoid him, she needed to increase her face time by stopping by to chat and connecting in one-on-one meetings. Eventually, she would need to make an effective pitch for a promotion. (If these tactics didn't work, Plan B was to find a new position.)

An important concern was building visibility and relationships with a wider group of executives. One of her strategies was to invite colleagues to speak to her team at a monthly "Lunch and Learn." It was valuable for her team to learn about other business areas, but it was even more valuable to Liz for the business contacts.

To tackle her meeting and presenting phobias, Liz joined Toast Masters and took courses on presentation skills. At first, she didn't feel self-confident, so she had to "fake it until you make it" until she found her voice, her power, and her style. She became a woman who brands.

You're Not a Man

The conventional wisdom has been that women have trouble succeeding because they don't act like men, the top-selling brand in the career marketplace. So the advice we've been given is to try to act like men. We took courses and tried to be more assertive. In the past, we were even encouraged to "dress for success," which meant dressing like a man, so we turned to dark, skirted suits with shoulder pads, briefcases, and tie-like scarves. Or we tried to adopt the male command-and-control model. Or we tried to model ourselves after male leaders in our company.

If that's the conventional wisdom, it's wrong. Playing it like a man doesn't work. Acting like a man brands you as tough and aggressive. When women adopt attitudes such as forcefulness and assertiveness, we can be lambasted as "too tough" and "unfeminine."

I remember a certain female executive back when I first worked on Wall Street. We'll call her "Alex." She was smart and got the job done, and done well. But her ideas on team building and compassion came right out of Joseph Stalin's playbook. Alex played the tough guy so well, you could imagine her as a fire-eater in the circus. She behaved like a bully and everyone was afraid of her, even her own staff. Alex represented what I hoped was a dying breed, a type not much discussed in women's leadership circles—the tough, successful female who is mean to other women and tries to sabotage them.

One day she called me to complain about a member of my staff, "Sophia," who had the audacity to disagree with the recommendation one of Alex's people had made in a meeting. And Alex complained to me about it in typical Alex fashion. "Tell your person if she does it again, I'll break her [expletive deleted] kneecaps."

Ouch! I didn't pass along Alex's stupid threat but counseled Sophia to always use all the diplomatic skills she could muster when talking with Alex or anyone on Alex's staff.

*   *   *

Bad behavior is disliked in a man.
But it's despised in a woman.

*   *   *

This sort of behavior is counterproductive and ultimately destructive. A few years later, as usually happens, Alex had a big project that blew up. She needed some supporters to rally around her and maybe put the blowup in perspective. Unfortunately for her, but fortunately for the company and everyone else, Alex had no supporters and left the firm. The reign of terror was over, and we all gave a big sigh of relief. Her bad reputation was so well known in the industry that she was never able to land a big job again.

Be Who You Are—A Woman

Trying to act like a man is stupid for the most basic reason. We're not men! And that's an advantage!

It's common sense to be authentic, and it's smart branding. Great commercial brands are always built on authenticity and on a brand's inherent strengths, and it's the same with you. Your brand must come from who you are, what makes you tick, what your passions are, and what your strengths are, even what your biology dictates. Confidence comes from being comfortable in your own skin.

You'll avoid the stress of trying to be something you're not and constantly attempting to fix your shortcomings. You'll be worth more as well.

The choice is between increasing results using your aptitudes and assets or making minor improvements to weak areas that will probably never be a major strength. Your house of cards may eventually collapse around you. Don't shortchange your assets and your power.

Nurture What You Want to Grow

So many things shape us—our family and friends, the education we receive, and the times we grow up in, along with our biology, our evolutionary history, and our genes.

The interesting thing is that what we nurture is what grows in us. And neuroscientists are proving it. Scientists talk of "neuroplasticity"—how what we experience and focus on can actually "sculpt" the shape, size, and number of neurons, even the thickness of the connections between them. It's like Mom always said: "Use it or lose it."

Many of us begin with great callings and then move on to duties and demands. But often we're great at managing priorities—at least, everyone's priorities but our own.

We need to put ourselves and our career success back into the equation. We need to leverage our personal strengths and our aptitudes as women. It's not helpful to blame the old boys' network or the glass ceiling. We need to focus on what we can control and on our best assets—our personal strengths and the aptitudes we're wired for as women.

The goal is to be ourselves, have fun, and succeed, and maybe even make the world a little better place.

We can't do these things unless we learn how to brand ourselves authentically. The most important asset you have is you. It's something that no one can take away from you. Your brand is your best self. Give it all the best things you want to be known for. You'll find that knowing your value is empowering personally, and others will perceive you differently. When you take charge of your career destiny, you'll be able to harness all the parts of yourself that contribute to your business success. You'll become a Woman Who Brands.

A WOMAN'S PLACE IS IN THE HOUSE (AND IN THE SENATE)

Kirsten Gillibrand
U.S. Senate, New York

Being elected to the United States House of Representatives and later being elected to the U.S. Senate have been unparalleled honors. I had long dreamed of doing public service, but to represent our New York families in Congress has been more exciting and more rewarding than I could have ever imagined.

My story began long before I was born, with a family of strong, accomplished women who would be my inspiration. Many today still think of women in government as unusual, but in my grandmother's time it was virtually unheard of. In a time when the ink was barely dry on the Nineteenth Amendment giving women the right to vote, my grandmother was involved in politics and advocated that women's voices be heard.

Starting in the late 1930s, my grandmother Dorothea "Polly" McLean Noonan was a secretary in the New York State Legislature in Albany. At the time, all the secretaries were women and nearly all of the legislators were men. My grandmother wanted to be involved not only in legislation and government but in the politics of the day.

She believed women should have a stronger voice in who represented them and their families, so she began to organize at the grassroots level. She helped lead the effort to organize the women of the legislature and then broadened the network of women to form the first Women's Democratic Club in the county of Albany.

My grandmother taught me the importance of broad-based activism. I watched her engage women at every level of the political process, from going door to door, staffing phone banks, and stuffing envelopes to encouraging them to be stronger advocates. Because of her commitment and leadership, women's voices were heard, and they made a difference in the agenda of the day.

One of the greatest gifts my grandmother gave me was simply taking me with her. I remember many fall afternoons as a young girl passing out flyers, putting bumper stickers on cars, and sitting in campaign headquarters stuffing envelopes in the company of many fascinating women.

I had another strong role model—my mother, Polly Noonan Rutnik. She also was a trailblazer and set out to make a difference as a lawyer when few women chose such a profession. She was one of only three women in her law school class, and her experiences were pretty shocking. She had a criminal law exam scheduled for the day she went into labor with my older brother. Being progressive, her law professor was gracious enough to let her take the exam the next day!

As an attorney, my mom became an advocate for families adopting children, buying their first homes, and drawing up wills. I became a lawyer because I wanted to learn how to be the strongest and most effective advocate I could be.

As a young lawyer, I soon became interested in getting involved politically. I followed in my grandmother's footsteps and began to organize women. I became involved in the Women's Leadership Forum, a national organization founded to engage women in presidential politics.

There were very few women under the age of forty involved, so I set out to change that. I founded a local Women's Leadership Forum network. We taught younger women how to organize, raise money, and be more effective issues advocates. I began to think about doing public service full-time but did not really know how to make that transition.

One day, I was at a Women's Leadership Forum event and Andrew Cuomo, secretary of the Department of Housing and Urban Development (HUD), was giving a speech about the importance of public service. After his talk, I approached him, introduced myself, and told him about my interest in serving, and he asked me to come to Washington to interview for a position as special counsel. After the interview, Mr. Cuomo offered me the job, and I accepted.

As special counsel at HUD, I was able to work on legislation that I thought mattered—such as the New Markets Initiative, intended to invest public and private money in low-income areas to build infrastructure and affordable homes. But mostly, it solidified my interest in doing public service full-time. Over the next few years, I thought about where I could best serve and decided that my training would lend itself best to serving at the federal level as a member of Congress.

In the meantime, my husband and I decided to raise our family where I had grown up, near my parents, brother's family, aunts, uncles, and cousins, in upstate New York. Once upstate, we decided that it was time to try to make that shift to full-time public service. I ran for the U.S. Congress representing the 20th District of New York.

I was privileged to win the seat and the great honor of representing more than 600,000 upstate New Yorkers in Washington. In 2009, I was appointed by Governor Paterson to fill the U.S. Senate seat formerly held by Hillary Clinton, and was elected in a special election for the seat held in 2010. I stay in touch with my constituents by holding town hall "Congress on your Corner" meetings at grocery stores, coffee shops, bookstores, and community centers, where I talk to folks about the issues that matter to them. I usually learn a tremendous amount and often get the best ideas for legislation directly from my constituents at these gatherings.

I hope to be a role model for young women, as my mother and grandmother were for me. I hope we will see more women in local and national office because they can see it is possible. I know my grandmother would be proud of me and of all the women who work every day to provide for their families and make a difference in their own special way.

Women who brand know
that if you don't brand yourself,
someone else will, and it won't be *your* brand.

2

BRAND YOURSELF FOR SUCCESS

A branding maven once said, "There is no 'and' in 'brand.'" Of course, the letters are there, but the advice means that you shouldn't define yourself as an accountant and an actress and an interior designer, as someone once described herself to me at a networking event.

Being a "this and that" person may be interesting on the cocktail party circuit, but it's a temptation you must be careful to avoid. You'll be much more successful with your career identity if you let go of extraneous portions of your identity to focus on a singular brand. Otherwise, people won't know what to make of you. You risk being branded "Jill of All Trades, Master of None." That's why it pays to be familiar with the basics of Branding 101.

Self-branding means being able to articulate a simple, clear expression of who you are, doing it consistently, and delivering on it again and again, so that when people think of X, they think of you. Or when people think of you, they think of X.

Some women, concerned with authenticity, think branding is fake. But good branding is always built on authenticity, although it's a simplified you that emphasizes what's most valuable about your many aptitudes. All the complexity of who you are is too confusing.

When you start thinking of yourself as a brand, you discover how powerful it can be. Rather than being viewed generically as one of the worker bees, you'll be someone who stands for something distinct and desirable—a brand.

✳ ✳ ✳

A self-brand is an identity that
sticks like peanut butter in the minds of others.

✳ ✳ ✳

In today's overcommunicated society, the brands that stand for something relevant and build positive perceptions are the ones that succeed. It's the same with people. In today's overcompetitive society, people who build a career identity—a personal brand—that has relevance and visibility in the marketplace will have the advantage.

That's why marketers figure out the big idea they can best use to leverage a brand, drum away at it consistently, and evolve it slowly over time.

Branding Is as Simple as 1, 2, 3

How do you figure out your brand idea and game plan for success? At its core, branding is a simple three-step process, and the following steps offer a good playbook for you to use in branding and marketing yourself successfully.

Step 1: Finding Your Brand Idea

To find your brand idea or USP (unique selling proposition), forget your job title and figure out how you add distinct value. Do a brand audit, like those marketers do, beginning with a SWOT Analysis looking at your strengths and weaknesses against the opportunities and threats you face. Look at the "market research" you get in your yearly review and performance feedback. What qualities and abilities make you different, even better, than others? Try to capture your brand idea in a crisp sentence.

Step 2: "Packaging" Brand You

Packaging is important in personal branding because looking the part and projecting gravitas (visual identity) convey powerful messages about who you are and create perceptions about what you can do. Likewise, your communications ability and the ideas and initiatives associated with you (verbal identity) can brand you as management material or cast you in the lower ranks.

Step 3: Marketing Brand You

Marketing is everything you do to build relationships and convey positive perceptions to your "customers" at every point where you come into contact with others. It means having a marketing plan of specific actions you are going to take to achieve short-term and long-term goals and measuring how you are doing.

So let's look at how you can find the best positioning idea, or USP (unique selling proposition), for Brand You.

Vive la Difference

The cardinal rule of branding is to be different. Being just like everyone else will stunt your success. You'll be anonymous—like a mass-produced person who's indistinguishable from others on the assembly line. People will define you in terms of others, and as a clone, you'll always be a B player.

Some people begin developing a self-brand by modeling themselves after successful people they admire, often people in their company. This has always been somewhat of a dilemma for women because there aren't a lot of female role models.

But even if you do look to others for ideas on how to model your brand, you always have to take it a step further. You have to refashion your brand based on what's authentic and different about you. You need to be yourself but stretch. You have to struggle against conformity if you want to find your own identity. After all, as Walt Whitman told us, "What you are, picks its way."

You need to figure out your own big idea—what's different, relevant, and special about you—so that you can compete in today's flat world. To do that, begin the traditional branding process with a brand audit, an analysis of the brand and key competitors. Part of the brand audit is the SWOT (strengths, weaknesses, opportunities, threats) Analysis.

Another approach marketers use is to think in terms of metaphor or analogy. What's different about a product (or you) may be difficult to explain and requires time for people to digest. But if you use a metaphor, anchoring the brand in something people already know, you short-circuit the process and enhance the brand's appeal. The key is to "anchor and twist"—anchor the idea in something familiar but give it your own twist, like Apple did with the iPhone. You don't want to be an imitator; you want to be like "*X* on steroids," or "a cross between *X* and *Y*," or "like *A* meets *B*."

You can also link different strengths to create your big idea. Look at Scott Adams, the creator of *Dilbert*. It's hard to be truly brilliant at one thing, but almost everybody, Adams feels, can be in the top 25 percent of two or even three things. And that's what he did in forming his own brand. Adams strung together drawing (he was a good but not a great artist), business savvy (not great at office politics but a good observer), and humor. He was in the top 25 percent in these attributes, but when he put them together, he created a powerful unique selling proposition—and created *Dilbert*.

You can also look into in-person assessments or online tests like the *Strong Interest Inventory*® instrument. Assessments and personality inventories can be a great starting point on your personal brand journey. But don't expect an instrument to tell you who you are and what you should do. None can do that. If you can stack up your passions on top of your natural talents, you can zero in on what you're good at and how you add value.

Be a Value Creator or a Game Changer

If you're seen as a value creator or a game changer, your brand will always be in demand. Companies want game changers, people who see a new trend when it is just a weak signal no one else notices. Being a game changer is a rare talent and a high risk–high reward personal brand positioning. Mark Zuckerberg and Jack Dorsey are both game changers in technology. With the dramatic success of her book, *Lean In*, Sheryl Sandburg became a game changer in female leadership and shot her personal brand into the business celebrity stratosphere. Being a game changer can supercharge your personal brand too, if you're a truly innovative thinker.

Being perceived as a value creator will also do wonders for your brand. And there's a lot of ways to create value. "Meg," who works in sales at a large media company, created value by coming up with a solution to a long-standing problem at her company. Her division, like the others in her company, worked in a silo, so it was difficult to put together cross-platform media packages custom tailored to the needs of individual clients as competitors were doing. Over time, the company was starting to lose business to more nimble, less siloed companies.

Meg proposed a monthly Innovative Client Solutions Summit, at which different cross-department teams would get together to come up with integrated and innovative solutions for clients. Meg set up metrics to measure follow-through and accountability, and proposed that part of each division's compensation would be based on successful multi-division projects.

Branders think of owning a word or phrase, and the phrase that Meg wanted her brand to own was "creator of innovative client solutions." It was a brand positioning that she was uniquely qualified to be associated with, as she had launched the monthly innovation summit and developed metrics to measure the success of cross-platform projects. Meg's brand idea, or USP, was a different idea that created enormous value for the company and for her career identity in the company.

What's Your Brand in a Sentence?

The branding process is simple, but it takes some strategic and creative thinking to come up with your unique idea of what you stand for. Your big idea should give people a reason to choose you and not the other person.

You should be able to articulate your brand idea in a crisp positioning sentence that conveys what's different and special about you in comparison with others and why it matters. It's something you'll use in pitching yourself for a promotion or a stretch assignment or in more casual networking situations.

One client defines her brand as "a bridge between strategy and execution," and gives examples that demonstrate her ability to come up with big ideas in her department and to execute them as well. A data analyst at a consumer products company who's great at understanding the story behind the numbers defines her brand as a "market researcher who can separate the signal from the noise." One way to define your brand is by linking two different things. For example, I call myself a personal brand strategist, a cross between a career coach and a Procter & Gamble brand manager.

Now we're ready to explore "packaging" your brand idea and the power of visual and verbal identity.

Your Name and Communications Ability as Verbal Identity

Today, having an unusual first name or last name is an advantage because you'll be easy to find in a Google search. Kanye West and Kim Kardashian were especially creative in naming their daughter North. So it's not surprising that for many parents today, unusual names are all the rage. "Baby names" has long been a top Internet search term, ranking up there with "weather" and "directions."

Most men don't change their last names when they get married, but women do all the time and they have a lot of choices. You can keep your name. You can hyphenate or not hyphenate. You can lose your maiden name completely. Look at Martha Kostyra. She took her husband's last name when she got married, and it was a smart move from a branding perspective. Would she have had the same success if she had kept her maiden name and called her media and home products empire Martha Kostyra Living? Maybe. Maybe not.

❋   ❋   ❋

Verbal identity: Your name and communications ability—
the way you define yourself verbally and the words, phrases,
and ideas associated with Brand You.

❋   ❋   ❋

Unless you have a name like Morgan, Alex, or Sandy, your first name betrays your gender, and that can affect people's perceptions about you as a businessperson. In a study at Harvard Business School, one group of students was asked to evaluate a case study of a venture capitalist named Heidi, and another group was asked to evaluate the same case study with one modification; the VC's name was changed from Heidi to Howard. You probably won't be surprised to hear that Howard was more "appealing" and Heidi was branded as "selfish," even though both groups of students consisted of men and women and the case study was identical except for the name switch.

As a brander, you'll want to become a strong communicator who not only presents ideas well in meetings, but who names her ideas and tells stories so that business accomplishments are seared in the minds of the audience.

Visuals Convey Powerful Messages

The complement to verbal identity in brand building is visual identity. It's no wonder branders pay a lot of attention to product style and packaging. Each brand aims for a distinctive look and packaging because visual identity can make a dramatic difference in product appeal. A company takes its brand's big idea and name and packages them so that everything works together to create a powerful brand statement.

And the importance of packaging is good for us women since we have an advantage in visual identity: We're nicer to look at! (George Clooney and Brad Pitt excepted.)

Women have a bigger arsenal of tools to work with. Unlike men, we have a wide range of options in clothing, color, hairstyles, accessories, and makeup, so it's easier to develop a memorable personal style that makes us stand out and get recognized as people or as leaders. And having attention-getting packaging is powerful. In the product world, a lively, colorful package makes consumers think its volume is bigger.

Likewise, clothes are messages, and looking the part will give you a boost in gravitas, self-confidence, and other positive associations. Of course, having more options in terms of how we dress means women have more opportunities to brand themselves well or bomb. Some women try to convey authority with a very tailored "I mean business" look, but it can come across as too severe rather than having the desired effect. In day-to-day meetings and presentations, it's important to convey authority but also femininity and warmth. The other, perhaps worse, wardrobe mistake is to look like you're dressed for a dinner date, not the corner office. A too-casual or evening look does not communicate the authority expected of a leader.

❋   ❋   ❋

Visual identity: Your distinct look, style, and demeanor—all the visual messages that communicate your brand nonverbally.

❋   ❋   ❋

There are a lot of different ways to convey authority and yet stay true to your style as a woman. Look at Angela Merkel, the German Chancellor. Known for her brightly colored jackets and her no-nonsense, let's-solve-the-problem leadership style, she communicates gravitas but also a nurturing women's sensibility, like a beloved mother or aunt.

Now that we've got our brand idea and verbal identity and visual identity in place, we're ready to go to market.

Marketing Brand You

Marketing Brand You is everything you do to promote yourself and build options and opportunities: a track record of experiences and achievements, visibility for yourself and your achievements, and strategic relationships and alliances. Even if you do nothing, you're doing something. You're ceding control of your brand to others.

Look at this story told by Sharon Allen, former CEO of Deloitte. Early in her career, Allen was surprised to see that her name wasn't on the list of newly promoted employees. She stewed about it, then decided to talk to her boss. Allen recounted how she had done A, B, C, and D over the last year, so she was surprised that her name wasn't on the list. Her boss said, "Sharon, I didn't know you did all of those things. You never told me." As Allen reminisced about this experience years later, she said, "It was a mistake that I never made again."

Think in Terms of Markets

As a self-brander, you'll need to define and prioritize your target markets just as marketers do. If you work in a company, your boss is your key target market, followed by other senior executives. These are the people who have the most power over your brand. So let's designate them your primary target market.

Your secondary target market will likely include colleagues, clients, your network, and your staff. Their thoughts about you will also play an important role in your success. With all your target audiences, you need to drill down and figure out what their problem is or what their need is first. Then, determine how you can solve their problem or fill that need.

In branding, we say "pick an enemy," meaning, if you want to figure out who your brand is for, you first have to decide who it's not for. Look at the Apple computer ad campaign with the hip Mac guy in jeans on the right and the nerdy PC guy on the left. It's clear who the target market is and who it isn't.

It's the same with people. You should realize that you won't be some people's cup of tea. If you try to appeal to everyone, you end up appealing to no one. The fear of being disliked has driven some women to try to appeal to everyone, and it's a major branding mistake. The "I want everyone to like me" approach doesn't work. Leaders have to be willing to turn some people off. But you want to build a large community with the rest, your brand community.

Some key colleagues at work who are not your target market will be your competitors. Not that you need to dislike them. In fact, you may admire them. You may learn new tricks from them. But you do have to figure out how to compete effectively, demonstrate the special aptitudes you bring to the party, and market your difference. You may even want to form alliances with some of your competitors—alliances are always a very smart brand move.

The Game Plan of a Woman Who Brands

The three-step branding process will help you think and act like a brand. You'll find that applying branding principles will give you an edge.

To succeed you need to create a powerful brand identity—a female brand identity—one that is authentically you and will help get you noticed and viewed positively in the career marketplace. You need to take charge of your brand, your career, and your life.

Explore individual female aptitudes and learn how to build on your strengths. Successful brands, after all, build on strengths and deflect attention from their weaknesses.

You'll also need to deal with preconceptions and biases. Understanding attitudes is core to smart branding, whether for a product or a person. If you understand what people think, you can change perceptions through artful persuasion in the messages (visual and verbal) and experiences you send out. After all, it's not who you think you are and what you can do that's so important. It's who other people think you are and what they think you can do that's so important.

None of us works in a vacuum, just as none of us works on a completely level playing field. But understanding and leveraging our strengths against the needs and perceptions in the career landscape will help us build a powerful personal brand identity.

After all, no matter who you are, your brand reputation arrives before you do. Either you have a personal brand identity that people are aware of or they draw a blank.

NOT A DAMSEL IN DISTRESS

Paula Forman
former president, Wells, Rich, Greene

My mother was one of the women to whom the book *The Feminine Mystique* spoke so profoundly. For her, the traditional female role was sadly incomplete.

I guess you could say that my apple fell close to her tree because I always knew I would have a career. I earned a PhD in sociology, yet I wound up on Madison Avenue, juggling a family, two kids, and a high-profile advertising job.

I don't understand today's young women. It seems they don't want to be like us. Many are willing to drop their careers when they get married or have kids. I would feel terrible if I had to ask my husband if I wanted to spend some money.

I want my own money.

Many women today prefer to stay in safe "women-type" jobs or think the workplace will accommodate them with flextime or schedules built around dropping off the kids. Who would hire them in a competitive industry?

Advertising is a competitive, collaborative process. You need to be available, not on the mommy track. If you aren't fully committed, you'll never get promoted. And when times turn tough, you'll be out altogether. Women and children overboard first.

I was always paid a lot, and for me that's important. I made sure the women I trained understood their worth, and I made sure they were paid well, too. I'm proud of that.

I think a factor in my success is that I took a big risk early on. I signed up to work on a big brand in major trouble at an ad agency. Colleagues warned me that it would destroy my career. Even my husband said, "No man would take that job."

But it didn't work out that way. Working with a strong partner and with my client, we turned the brand around.

I built a reputation very fast that way.

As a woman leader, you have to be self-aware and know how you're coming across. You need to learn how to play it—learn to have some idea of what you can and can't get away with. I am small in stature, and that gave me license to be large in my behavior, to be a charismatic leader.

Women have a more personal style in business, and that's an advantage. A woman's strength is in creating relationships. Men more often create distances. You need to create a personal feeling, a personal style as a leader. That was a big factor in my success.

Of course, on the other hand, you can be too personal also. You don't want to be everyone's best friend. I burned myself out by having five hundred intimate relationships when I was president of Wells, Rich, Greene.

I'll always remember a telling moment toward the end of my time at the ad agency. The CEO and I had some kind of knock-down, drag-out over something. He was screaming and yelling, and it became very threatening.

When I finally got out of his office, there were two creative guys standing there, and I said, "Why didn't you call 911 or something to try to save me?"

"Save you? You're the president of the company, not a damsel in distress!"

Women who brand use emotional intelligence as a powerful business tool to connect with others and gain insight by "reading" nonverbal clues.

3

EMOTIONAL INTELLIGENCE GIVES WOMEN AN EDGE

Let's face it, the business world is as much a personality contest as high school ever was. Likeability is especially important for women. You may get hired on performance and credentials, but it's hard to get promoted if you're not liked. And you have to make more of an effort to connect with others and avoid an all-business approach as you become more successful. Success and likeability are positively correlated for men and negatively correlated for women.

So what are the components of likeability? Well, *attractiveness* counts, but you don't want to be too attractive or it will work against you. You want to tap into the *similarity* principle. People like people who they think are like the person they see in the mirror every day, someone they can imagine having a beer with. And finally, you want to be *authentic*. It's hard to like someone you feel is a phony, earnestly trying to be something she's not.

You'll find that the most likeable people aren't perfect at all. They are comfortable in their own skin and they're not afraid to show vulnerability. In fact, many extremely successful women realize that showing vulnerability can be a strength in business because it makes them human and it's easier for people to relate to them.

Look at Oprah Winfrey. Even though she's worth hundreds of millions, she's not afraid to reveal her struggles with her weight and easily empathizes with her guests' problems no matter their situation.

Then there's the actress Jennifer Lawrence. It's not so easy to "like" someone who won an Academy Award at age twenty-two, but she charmed everyone as she stumbled her way to the stage and gave a candid, self-effacing acceptance speech. Rather than seeming excessively coached in the Hollywood mode, she is the unHollywood actress. She calls herself "uneducated," loves a Budweiser rather than the hot indie brew of the moment, and talks about her addiction to *Keeping up with the Kardashians* and being starstruck meeting Jack Nicholson. Sounds more like the girl next door than the hottest female actress on the planet.

Boost Your Q Score

In branding, as in life, being liked counts a lot. That's why marketers look at a celebrity's Q Score if they are considering someone for a TV commercial or endorsement contract. The Q Score is a numerical rating of a celebrity's familiarity and appeal. People with a high Q Score have strong brand equity: they are well known and well liked.

Marketers are looking for the celebrity's likability to rub off onto their brand and create an emotional bond with consumers. Julia Roberts and Tom Hanks are not paid top dollar for starring in movies just because they are famous or are great actors. One could argue that they are not even the best in terms of acting ability, but they do have very high Q Scores, which means they are well known and extremely well liked by lots of people.

It's almost as if the celebrities with high Q Scores seem close to the person we see in the bathroom mirror each morning. We see them as sharing our values and life experiences. We feel a rapport with them, almost as if they are our friends. And the higher the Q Score, the higher the salaries stars get paid for movies or product endorsements.

We've got a Q Score, too, but not the kind celebrities have, that you can find on a list. We're sized up, too, in terms of visibility, personality, and appeal and are compared to other people on these measures. Having a high Q Score will make us more successful, and we can take it to the bank, too.

So, how can you make yourself more likable and appealing?

Create a Comfort Connection

In many ways, brands are like people and people are like brands. An important concept today is *emotional branding.* People buy brands that they like and connect with, not necessarily the brands that they've analyzed and decided are superior. That's why brand personality is so important. When marketers prepare a creative brief on a brand, they often list personality traits or descriptive adjectives for it, or prepare a brand persona as if the brand were a person with a personality and point of view.

Personality is essential for your brand, too. That's why it's important to let people know you beyond the corporate ID. It's hard to be likable when you come across as more corporate automaton than human. Some women, feeling insecure as they operate in a male world, come across as stiff and overly professional. Realize that the corporation is not you, and don't let an overemphasis on work make you appear cold and too serious.

As women, we also have a powerful mechanism for using emotional branding to increase our personal appeal. It's our exceptional power of empathy.

Empathy is the ability to step into another person's shoes and quickly pick up on his or her pain, joy, or other feelings and respond with a similar emotion. It's the ability to relate to someone by finding an attitude of similarity, and when people think we like them, they like us. Most experts in gender research seem to agree that women have an edge over men in empathy. But writers on gender who don't like the idea of male–female differences find the topic disagreeable because they associate empathy with women's caregiving role as mothers. That view is too narrow. Empathy is not only a powerful biological instinct; it can be a powerful career and social tool.

Empathy is based on finding similarities between ourselves and someone else, and this ability is a driving force in human behavior. We are attracted to people who are similar to us in some way: similar beliefs, similar looks, even similar names and birth dates. When people are similar to us, we give them special status, like wanting to do business with them or help them out.

❋   ❋   ❋

*Empathy: Finding a comfort connection
with others through a sense of similarity.*

●   ●   ●

Empathetic people find areas of common ground with the other person by mirroring his or her feelings and actions. Smart empathizers look for things to like in other people, and when people feel that you like them, they like you. In relationship building, don't look for differences– look for similarities. Find things to like about others and you will be surprised at the result.

Wired for Empathy

There's a reason why we're moved to tears so easily by movies. It's often involuntary. Science has unveiled a powerful unconscious mind that processes nonverbal communication, emotions, and all kinds of other unspoken clues and allows us to understand and connect with others. Recently, scientists discovered a different type of brain cell called the mirror neuron. These cells act like mirrors that reflect back to us what others are feeling or doing and are the roots of our empathy.

There are also assessments for empathy, like the PONS (Profile of Nonverbal Sensitivity) test, which measures people's ability to read and relate to nonverbal clues. Simon Baron-Cohen developed the EQ (Empathy Quotient) test, which showed that women score higher in identifying the feelings of others and were more easily influenced by other people's feelings.

MRI and PET scans show that women process emotional pictures through different brain networks than men use. Most women use both hemispheres of the brain (men use one) and have more activity in the amygdala, the core emotional area in the brain. And we have a thicker connection between the two brain hemispheres. In short, our brains are designed for emotional connection. Emotions seem to take up more brain area and have more efficient means of transport. So it's not surprising that women can quickly pick up and accurately read emotional messages that leave men clueless.

And what a powerful tool that is. Women can call up memories with greater intensity than men can. We are better than men at reading faces and can quickly distinguish between facial expressions of happiness, anger, fear, and sadness. We also surpass men in the ability to tell whether something is authentic or artificial.

Women also are more apt to reach out to someone for emotional connection in times of stress. Genes and hormones such as estrogen and oxytocin power our emotional sensitivity and drive our interest in social connections and emotional involvement. Like all good things, though, empathy has a downside. Women are more likely to feel sadness and anxiety and are twice as likely as men to suffer from depression.

That new class of recently discovered brain cells called mirror neurons helps women understand immediately the thoughts, actions, and intentions of others. One neuroscientist predicted that "mirror neurons will do for psychology what DNA did for biology." The brain has multiple mirror neuron systems that help with reading people, mimicking actions, reading someone's intentions, determining the social implications of an action, and reading emotions.

The same brain areas that are active when a person feels pain or pleasure also are activated when that person imagines someone else feeling the same pain or pleasure. When you identify with a character on television or in a movie, the mirror-neuron activity that lights up on MRI scans suggests that you are actually living the actor's role and experiencing the story taking place on the screen through your motor neurons. And it all happens very quickly, in a fraction of a second. It's these unconscious perceptions and identification with what others are feeling that help us understand them.

Go with Your Gut

Like empathy, intuition gives you information that you can choose to act on or not. It's a powerful form of intelligence. It gives us powerul abilities in social perception.

Intuition is not some airy-fairy hunch machine but a neurologically based behavior that developed so we could sense and quickly respond to danger. In essence, we can know more through our gut than through our minds. When we go with our gut, we discern what's really going on, not through reason or analysis of facts, but through our unconscious minds. Often, our gut opinion—what comes to mind first—is the best one, far better than what we think of after considered analysis.

Your unconscious mind is a great resource for finding solutions that elude you during the day. Some people get their best work-related ideas while driving, others while showering, but sleep seems to be a great place to achieve breakthroughs. When we sleep, our brains try to connect the dots and explore ideas in a trial-and-error fashion, experiments show, making it easier to bridge the gaps and solve the dilemma.

We all have scanning patterns. Our antennae are up to spot certain types of clues and information. What we want to do is to increase our radar range so that we can pick up more. You'll find that the more you do it, the better you will be, and that your gut instincts are often right. Likewise, you can send out scanning patterns to mold a company culture as well. If you're the boss and walk around the halls to stay in touch, pretty soon you'll see a lot more people walking around and dropping in unannounced.

Women are good at spotting a lie, and MRI brain studies show that there is truth to the expression "something smells fishy." The area in the brain that lights up when we hear a false statement is the same area that lights up when we smell something bad. A different area of the brain lights up when someone says something that we believe is true.

✹   ✹   ✹

Intuition is the sense of knowing something
immediately without reasoning.

✹   ✹   ✹

"Leslie," a female executive at a major accounting firm, told me about a group conference call with two other partners and an important new client, a woman. The client mentioned that her daughter had just left for college and then the conference call proceeded with its agenda.

Leslie sensed immediately that something was amiss and wondered to herself, "Gee, should I say anything? I don't know her at all." But at the end of the call she said, "It must be tough being an empty nester. My child just went off to kindergarten today, and I feel a sense of loss, and it's just kindergarten."

Afterward, Leslie's partners told her, "You have just added more value than we could have in building a relationship with this client." The important thing is to have the courage to act on your intuition when you feel something strongly.

Observe Boys and Girls

This feminine edge in social and emotional intelligence—in correctly reading nonverbal clues—begins early and continues throughout our lives. In his book *The Essential Difference,* Simon Baron-Cohen draws this basic distinction between the female and male ways of making sense of the larger culture. Women use a people-based way (empathy), while men use an object-based way (understanding and building systems).

Our empathetic ability starts young. Even girls as young as a year old respond more to the emotions of others and sympathize more. This empathetic ability continues into preschool. Studies show that pre-school girls have a stronger idea than boys of what's going on emotion-ally in stories. Little girls make sad faces and comforting sounds when they encounter a sad story.

Both ways have advantages. Empathizing gives you a powerful tool for understanding people and society. Systematizing gives you a powerful tool for understanding how the culture's organizations work.

Of course, we all have both abilities, but as a rule, women favor the feeling and empathizing route because it's second nature and the stronger aptitude. And empathizing is a great branding tool because it helps you connect with others emotionally. That's what brands strive for.

Emotional Branding

Emotional branding plays a big role in persuasion in advertising and sales. Again, it's the power of feelings over thinking. Marketers try to lock in their brands with consumers with messages that appeal to the heart. Star salespeople use emotional branding instinctively. They are apt to connect emotionally by subtly mimicking the rhythm and move-ments of the other person to create rapport and a rapid emotional bond.

Just a smile can make a big difference in building an emotional connection. It will lift your spirits and everyone else's, too. (My mom was always telling me to smile. Wasn't yours?) Smiling is a powerful nonverbal social and business tool. Our brains prefer happy faces. MRI scans show that our brains light up when we see a happy face. It's what scientists dub the "happy face advantage," so give people what will make their brains happy and you'll look better at the same time.

＊　＊　＊

Emotional branding: Differentiating your brand by building emotional connections with your "customers."

＊　＊　＊

Moods, like smiles, are contagious. It's all part of what social scientists call "primitive emotional contagion." Our positive energy energizes others and us. In fact, positive energy is one of the consistent traits of leaders. When we're around positive, successful people, it makes us feel positive and successful, too. It's an unconscious yet irresistible tendency to mimic other people's moods, expressions, and tone of voice, even their posture. A positive attitude is like a seed that germinates success. A negative attitude is like a virus that spreads failure.

Being around winners makes us feel like winners, too. And people perceived as winners get rewarded in our society: with bigger salaries, with awards, with contracts, with important relationships, with board seats. Likewise, negative energy is toxic. When we're around pessimistic people, it makes us want to cross over to the dark side, too. And if we're down, it will be harder for us to succeed. If you exude bad vibes, sooner or later you'll find yourself feeling even bleaker.

Be especially vigilant about the toxic messages you're sending to yourself by saying things like "Oh, stupid me" or "I haven't accomplished much." This sort of negative talk is self-defeating and will ultimately doom your brand. Rather than see limitation, believe it's an abundant world with lots of opportunity for you (because it is). People like positive, successful people and avoid negative people who don't appear to be doing well.

Like = Like

Scientists have been studying exactly how persuasive mimicry works. They're finding that persuasive people imitate another person's movements, even their rhythm and cadence, in a natural way. For example, if a customer makes deep eye contact, they reflect that back. If another customer favors quick glances, that is reflected back.

❋   ❋   ❋

Subtle imitation of another person
produces rapport with that person.

❋   ❋   ❋

Studies show that this subtle dance of words and gestures helps people click. People feel in sync with you unless they catch on and perceive you as being artificial. Persuasive mimicry works only if your moves seem natural and part of the conversation. There needs to be about a two-second delay. Employing these skills can help you get an almost immediate positive response even from someone you just met.

As the boss, what you communicate nonverbally has a powerful impact. In one study, a boss gave employees disastrous performance reviews but did it with a caring manner, and people rated the experience positively. Then the test was flip-flopped and the boss gave employees a positive message but did it with a frown. Even though the verbal message was positive, people felt worse than the employees in the first study who actually got bad news.

Perceptions Matter

When I was a child, my mother always told me, "Don't pay attention to what other kids say."

Boy, was that bad advice.

In business as well as in society in general, we need other people to think well of us. Our success is based on it. Just as in the branding world, everything in the career world is based on other people's perceptions. If people think you're management material, you will be. If they think you're a B player, you will be until you change their perceptions.

We receive feedback every day. We just need to tune in to it. Just look for the signs. Our empathy and intuition skills can help us see ourselves as others see us. We can tap into subtle shifts in mood.

Of course, if you work in a corporation, you're likely to get a formal review. But in today's politically correct workplaces, it may be hard to get honest feedback. Minority women have told me that they don't get good feedback and suspect that managers are afraid to critique them.

But there is a lot you can learn by using your powers of intuition and empathy. What perceptions do people have about you in the workplace? Do people come to sit near you at meetings? Do colleagues return your phone calls and e-mails? Are you invited to important meetings? What kinds of comments do you hear after you make a point? Do people drop by your office to chat?

From a branding perspective, perceptions are paramount. At its core, branding is about tuning in to and molding perceptions and, of course, changing perceptions.

Conduct Your Own Focus Group

Senior executives often get a 360-degree evaluation of how they are perceived by others. It's a confidential evaluation that seeks feedback from your boss and senior executives, colleagues and direct reports, clients, and even your spouse.

It's like a personal focus group.

Speaking as someone who's undergone a 360, it can be pretty tough medicine to read some of these anonymous comments. Most of us see ourselves through rose-colored glasses, and we can crash to earth pretty quickly. There's usually a grain (or more) of truth to the comments, even if someone does have an ax to grind. Throw out the outliers, but look for a consensus of opinion on how you come across. Don't obsess over the criticism; look at the good comments, too, and take action on what you learn.

You can also put together an informal focus group. Take a friend or colleague out to lunch or coffee and tell him or her that you are working on a personal branding project. But keep it light. Keep it fun. The person you've selected should be flattered.

✹   ✹   ✹

If you were a famous person, who would it be?
Ask your friends and colleagues what they think.

✹   ✹   ✹

Ask, "When you think of me and my personality, what comes to mind?" "If you were my brand manager, what advice would you give me on improving my brand?" "If there was one thing you would change about Brand Me, what would it be?" "If I were a famous person, who would it be? Why do you think that?" Now, try it with someone else.

Bosses and mentors can give you helpful advice on how you're coming across. I was relatively new at one company, and I said to my boss that I didn't feel part of the team that included her other direct reports. Her response bowled me over: "You come across as too perfect, too in control of all your projects, so your colleagues feel intimidated by you."

"Gee, isn't that what I should be doing?" I replied.

"Sure," she said, "but if you want to have a better relationship with your colleagues, show them your human side. Stop by their office to chat. Don't come across as perfect. Talk about how you messed up on something."

Even though I thought my job was to have my act together, I took her advice and started stopping by to chitchat with my colleagues from time to time instead of just focusing on work. I told them about difficulties I was facing. I even complained about my dating life— nonexistent at the time! And it worked. My relations with my colleagues improved dramatically after I became more human and less work focused.

This experience made me realize that what colleagues think about you is important, too. While your boss and other senior executives will be the primary ones to weigh in on promotions, positive word of mouth among the rank and file influences their opinion. Plus, you'll find it much easier to get cooperation on collaborative projects.

It's also important to eat a little humble pie if a self-review is part of your company's employee review process. A smart young woman on my team once gave herself a glowing review in a way that left no room for improvement. Now "Joan" was a terrific, hardworking, and talented person. I was very satisfied, but part of the game of self-reviews is to note areas for improvement. Otherwise, you come across as arrogant. You need to isolate some issues, and not the "I work too hard" variety that never seems genuine. Reveal some secret skill that you're working to improve. You'll steal the thunder of the person reviewing you and come across as candid and likable, and the flaw will be diminished in everyone's eyes.

Use Your Emotional Intelligence to Make Your Case

It may not be fair, but there are some perceptions about women that we need to deal with. High on the list is women asking for money. Women are notoriously bad at asking for more money for themselves. In one study of graduate students negotiating for their first jobs, 59 percent of the men asked for more money, but only 12.5 percent of the women did. And negotiating for more money paid off. Both the men and the women who asked for more received an average increase of 7.5 percent.

So, women should ask for more, right?

Well, many people—women and men—have a double standard. Studies show that women who asked for more money were viewed as "not nice," while men who did the same were not judged the worse for it. And both men and women who participated in the research had a negative opinion of women haggling.

One tactic that has worked well for me is to use humor in a negotiation, particularly a situational, self-deprecating comment like, "You know, you made a good point here, and I think my stubbornness is getting in the way of hearing what you are recommending." This should break the tension and lead to a more fruitful conversation. Another idea is to use your empathetic skills to find common ground and maybe even preempt the negotiating session with a bold volley.

While you want to fight for your rights, don't be a gender warrior. Victim talk is a very potent negative brand message, and it won't encourage most men and many women to empathize with you or like you better. I'm not saying that women haven't been taken advantage of, but we may have to see all the planets align before we snuff out all "unfair" gender attitudes. Rightly or wrongly, women hold many of the same gender attitudes that men hold. So a lot of reprogramming will need to take place. Everyone—male, female, black, white, or blue—has been a "victim" at some time. Carrying it around is like a personality flaw, thinking the glass is always half empty.

Building battle lines won't move you forward, whether the charge is gender bias or the glass ceiling. You will be spreading negative energy that will hurt, not aid, your career success. You'll be branded a shoulder-pad feminist or worse. And partnering with men in the career world is a much smarter way to go than engaging in the "battle of the sexes." It's important to realize that many work environments are receptive to women, so if you're not in one, make it your mission to find one. Even consider finding an internal champion among the senior ranks in your company and starting up a women's initiative as a positive force for change.

Leave the Tears at Home

It's happened to me. And it's probably happened to you. We can't and shouldn't stop ourselves from feeling or reacting emotionally.

After all, it's natural for women to express more emotion. Our desire to be more transparent about how we feel about a situation has brought a lot of concerns to the surface in the workplace. And that's good. Women are like the canary in the coal mine, as more than one woman executive told me.

But wearing your heart on your sleeve can be a problem. Crying is generally not smart in the workplace. Women may understand, but men have a hard time handling tears and may think you're not up to the job. So if you feel an emotional moment coming on, it's best to excuse yourself and go someplace private.

Often women react emotionally to a slight in the workplace, as "Melinda" did when her boss overlooked her for a promotion. What did Melinda do? She started avoiding her boss. She was holding a grudge, a bad strategy given that her boss had the most power over her brand and her promotion. Most men realize that it's not personal—it's business—and march right into the boss's office with five points on why they should have been promoted. And they don't leave before getting a timetable for what to do to advance.

* * *

Don't make the mistake of taking business slights personally.

* * *

Melinda, like many women, took the situation personally. She was hurt and didn't say anything to her boss. She started looking for another job. She was even composing a parting shot to lob at her boss as she walked out the door! Yet, she hadn't done the most basic thing—talk directly to her boss. It wasn't until she resisted those first impulses and met with her boss to outline her goals and accomplishments that she got what she wanted.

Emotional Tranquility

So how do you develop tactics for equanimity? It's especially hard when you want to scream "I'm out of here!" And in tough economic times, it can be even more challenging because everyone is under so much pressure. However, we only make it worse when we hold on to our responses to negative criticism and unfair treatment.

Here are four exercises to avoid holding on to unwanted feelings:

- **The Third Person:** Try to remove yourself from the situation mentally by imagining that you are an observer hovering over the scene. You might even smile inwardly at the business games some people play.
- **Teflon Shield:** Imagine that negative comments and experiences roll off of you like they would on a Teflon surface. (President Ronald Reagan was said to use this technique.)
- **The Magic Bubble:** Visualize your unwanted emotions and place them inside a big, radiant bubble and watch it float up in the sky and disappear.
- **The Circle:** Imagine a circle and invite the person you are having trouble with inside the circle. Visualize having a very calm conversation explaining your feelings and listening to the other person's point of view, then imagine both of you leaving the circle in a positive state of understanding.

While you don't want to come across as emotional, you also don't want to be seen as a cold, strictly business executive either. It's deadly branding for a woman. Some corporate women adopt the cool professional image as a way to fit in, particularly in male-heavy industries. But it's a trap, because when you come across as all corporate, it can make it hard for people to connect with you. That's why Hillary Clinton's emotional moment in New Hampshire during the 2008 primary, when she came close to tears, helped her with that state's women voters. They saw an authentic expression of emotion they could relate to. Clinton realized that showing more of who she is as a person was as important as articulating policy and adjusted her style going forward.

You Are You

You won't be successful building a strong emotional bond with professional associates unless you understand yourself. When you do, you'll be the kind of leader people are yearning for—a leader who will talk to them in a candid and open way, the kind who is willing to admit that she doesn't have all the answers but is committed to solving problems in an intelligent way.

Your authenticity is even more powerful when you have that extra spark, that extra something. In people, it's what the Spanish call "duende." Duende has been described as inspiration, magnetism, and charm. It's hard to define, but you know it when you feel it in someone. You sense their authenticity and understanding, energy and inspiration, like light coming out of darkness.

NOT LIVING IN AN IVORY TOWER

Deborah Elam
chief diversity officer, General Electric

Ivory towers may be fine for princesses in a storybook, but for the executive in the fairy tale of corporate life, I've learned that being approachable and candid are the strengths you need for success.

Although I have many more responsibilities, I feel I am the same person I was when I started out as an intern at GE twenty-one years ago. I think this attitude helps keep me from becoming isolated and losing touch with what's important—people.

Even as a young girl growing up in New Orleans, I gravitated toward leadership. I was a leader in Girl Scouts and the church choir, and the president of my high school class in both my freshman and senior years. But I value most the skills I learned playing competitive high school volleyball: teamwork, networking, strategy, focus, and hard work. These are the same skills required of a corporate exec!

These attributes can be acquired in various places, but sports competition is great training for leadership success, particularly for girls. That's one reason I encourage my two daughters to get out and compete on the ice rink. The other reason is that it's fun.

In college I became fascinated with the broader aspects of society and switched my major from premed to sociology. I still loved dealing with the individual but was fascinated with the macro as well as the micro aspects of society. How does culture evolve? How do individuals form their beliefs?

I joined the internship program at GE while earning my master's degree. I was in a two-year rotational program in human resources. This gave me wonderfully broad experience as I moved from aircraft engines to consumer finance, from Washington, DC, to Cincinnati, to Atlanta, to Raleigh, to Stamford, Connecticut.

This mobility was one key to my success: both the invaluable experience and my willingness to accept new and different challenges. I was single, loved to travel, and eager to take on new things.

Of course, as we mature, these attitudes often change, so it's important to take advantage of your youth. It's normal not to want to move every couple of years after you have a family and want some stability. Today, women need a career that fits us as well as we fit it.

Many African Americans like me took inspiration from Dr. Martin Luther King Jr., particularly his advice to be the best you can be no matter what you do. "If you're a street sweeper, be the best street sweeper you can be." This is true in life as well as in your career. Doing your absolute best builds leadership qualities and shows others that you have those abilities.

Networking needs to be a key part of your strategy for success. Many African American women have a natural skill set for building what I call "comfort connections." We find common ground with people, whether it is through kids, schools, sports, or business.

Most women are also good at cross-networking with women and men of varied backgrounds in varied settings. Too many people think of networking only with people like themselves. That's too limiting. You need to expand your horizons.

Another important strength is that women are great multitaskers. We have to be. We have full lives. We're executives, wives, and mothers. We're involved in the community. We have to be well organized and able to multitask and compartmentalize.

Continued success, of course, gets more difficult and subtle as you approach the very senior levels in business. By then, everyone is good at what they do. You need to get yourself "out of the pile," as Jack Welch put it. You need to be able to strategically focus on how you are adding value.

Women have often been good at giving credit to the team, but you need to credit both the team and your own role, too.

Success is both micro and macro—yourself and others. Though few make it to the top, those few cannot live in an ivory tower apart from people, who, after all, are as important to the company as anything else. It's important to value all the people you associate with.

When I was made the first African American female officer in GE's history, I received more than 350 e-mails from colleagues and well-wishers at every level in the company. I had to break my policy of answering all my e-mails within twenty-four hours. However, all 350 people did receive a heartfelt, personal, and very grateful thank-you.

Women who brand know the words
you use in business can be memorable
or blow away like packing peanuts in a hurricane.

4

FEMALE VERBAL AGILITY CAN GIVE YOU A COMMUNICATION HEAD START

Women have a verbal edge. It's strong across the board and starts at an early age. Girls generally start talking a month earlier than boys do and seem to use a larger vocabulary at an earlier age. Girls are better spellers and readers. Girls score better on verbal memory, or recall of words. Girls also have markedly stronger written language skills than boys. In one fascinating project, researchers studied two-year-old fraternal twins, each pair a boy and a girl. The twins shared the same parents and home environment and half of the same genes, yet the girls outdid the boys in vocabulary, hands down. And verbal agility is an advantage that stays with girls throughout the school years and beyond.

Communication = Power

The prowess we women have with spoken and written communication—our verbal edge—is a tool we can use for career success. After all, a big part of career success is based on this one simple, basic skill. Communication.

Commercial brands focus a lot of attention on brand message strategy and tactics: what to say and how to say it. And corporate icons, successful politicians, and celebrities do, too. It's important for you as well. It's hard to get the job in the first place unless you can communicate well, even in your first interview. Indeed, the skills that employers value most—the ability to communicate clearly and persuasively—are skills that new MBAs and college graduates often lack.

Communication is the glue that holds business relationships together. Expressing yourself well is imperative for selling your ideas in meetings and in presentations to large groups or for writing reports, letters, and e-mails. And the higher you go in the professional world, the more verbal agility can help you succeed, and piling on the "you knows" or "uhs" can brand you as not ready for prime time. The one trait most people at the top share is superior communication skills.

Wired to Communicate

As it does with our empathy edge, our brain architecture gives us an edge in verbal prowess, including both written *and* spoken aptitudes. Certain parts of the brain respond differently in women than in men during language tasks. Both the right and left hemispheres of the brain are activated in most women, while only the left hemisphere is activated in most men. Some gender experts speculate that there's a connection between our high empathetic skills and language agility.

Remember, the connection between the two hemispheres of the brain is thicker in women than it is in men. And that's not all. The female brain is densely packed with 11 percent more neurons in the language area. So women are wired to communicate, and how.

✻   ✻   ✻

Our unique brain network for language gives us an edge
in reading, writing, and speaking.

✻   ✻   ✻

Women have a rep for talking more and even faster than men, whether it's chatting endlessly with their women friends or not knowing when to shut up. Deserved? The results are mixed. For every study showing that women talk more and link our loquacity to a special "language" gene, there's another study that shows men talk more or that it's about even. Based on personal observation, I side with the women-talk-more camp and feel that our communications strength can be a tremendous asset as we learn how to use it to our advantage.

Girl Talk

It's not just the sound and higher pitch of a voice that brand it as female. Women have a different communication style. Because we're empathetic, we may speak in shorthand unless we catch ourselves.

A good friend of mine was working as a mortgage broker in a small office in Vermont. One day, his boss, a woman, stopped by his desk and started a conversation. "You live in Jericho, don't you? I wonder if you drive through Essex on your way home."

"No, not really," my friend replied. "I avoid Essex because of the traffic and use a great shortcut."

Over the next days and weeks, things got very strained between my friend and his boss. He was clueless as to why. Within three months, he was out the door.

What my friend didn't realize, and later learned from a former colleague, was that his boss's car had been in the repair shop in Essex, and that conversation was her subtle way of asking him for a lift so she could pick it up.

My friend thought the conversation was about driving routes. Guys talk about that all the time. She, being an empathetic female, thought he and everyone in the office knew she was having car problems. And she was furious because he wasn't willing to help her out.

It's the business version of "he said, she said." She thinks, "What's the matter with this jerk? Why won't he help me? And I'm his boss!" While he thinks, "She's just talking and not saying anything. Is there a point in there somewhere?"

Plain talk works best.

* * *

Girl talk—collaborative.
Guy talk—direct.

* * *

People need direct, clear-cut, unambiguous instructions, like "John, your team needs to figure out and fix the distribution logjam by the end of next week." Vague musings are not the direct, clear communication of a leader. As a communicator, you have a choice. You get to choose whether or not your audience will understand you by the way you say something. As Mom said, "Talking a lot doesn't mean you're communicating."

Beware of Low Power Talk

Women tend to use a verbal style called "mitigated" speech that is more collaborative and cooperative (Don't you think we should...") or that deals with disagreement in terms that make it easier to swallow ("I can see why you might think that, but..."). Mitigated speech is the polite, indirect talk that experts associate with a lower-power person talking to someone of higher status.

When they want to get a group to do something, women are more likely to use mitigated language and say, "Let's" or even just drop a hint ("I wonder if") like the female boss who wanted a ride, rather than exert their personal power and make a direct command or ask a clear, specific question. Men tend to have more hierarchical groups than girls and tend to use explicit language to get what they want, like "Give me" or "I want." Men also tend to challenge, disagree, and interrupt more.

While women's way of talking is more polite and community minded, it's not always the best communication choice. It depends upon the situation.

Let's look at the various degrees of mitigated language you might use in a professional situation with others:

1. **Command:** Strategy X is our plan.
2. **Obligation Statement:** We need to try strategy X.
3. **Suggestion:** Why don't we do strategy X?
4. **Question:** What do you think of strategy X?

5. **Preference:** Maybe we should look at one of these alternatives
6. **Hint:** I wonder if there are problems with our current plan.

The top three are high-power, command-and-control styles of communication associated with men or senior-ranking people. The bottom three examples of more mitigated speech are lower-power communication styles and tend to be favored by women or people of lower status.

Asking a question, seeking team consensus, or dropping a hint is certainly more polite and deferential than a command, and can be the best choice in certain situations. But mitigated language is inherently more confusing. What is the speaker trying to say? Where does she stand? What should we do?

In studies done of airline pilots, female captains tended to use an obligation statement like, "I think we need to deviate to the right now," while the male captains tended to use a direct command like, "Turn 30 degrees to the right." So the female captains in a leadership role were using a high-power style of communication, but they used number 2 on the scale, rather than the strongest, direct-command approach. They chose a softer way of speaking that was more inclusive of the team and consequently preferred by other crew members.

Listen, Really Listen

Listening is also a communication skill. People often don't listen. They just wait for an opening to talk. So they're taking turns talking, rather than listening when the other person is talking.

But listening, especially empathetic listening, is something that women have an edge with and can excel at with practice. It's very powerful because people realize that we are really listening and understanding their point of view. It's not something that comes naturally to most people, so we need to catch ourselves when we want to interrupt and give our opinion. In fact, the ability to really listen to other people—so that each one feels he or she is the most important person in our universe at that moment—is one trait often cited about well-liked leaders.

Listening is also a powerful persuasion tool. Many salespeople are coached to stop talking, ask questions, and listen. And it works.

Find *Your* Voice

As a self-brander, you'll want to capitalize on your verbal advantage by finding your own voice. Voice is about finding your own communication style, one that's authentic and distinctive to you.

Voice is about content, but it's also about how you express that content, even the sound of your voice. You want to find a voice that's true to your personality and point of view, that's confident and says things a little differently than others do. It's not just writing or speaking eloquently, though that's an asset. It's having your own way of connecting with others and expressing yourself. It's not easy to find your voice. Most people do it by trial and error, often combining various influences into something that's fresh and different. That's your voice and point of view.

The words you use and the stories you tell can be powerful and stick in the mind, or they can blow away like packing peanuts in a hurricane. Using a different word or expression slows people down so that they take notice, and it can linger in their minds when they think of you.

Politicians are pros at finding a voice. They want to link themselves with a word or idea that they can own in the public's mind, something that seals in their brand.

A huge chunk of Barack Obama's appeal in the 2008 presidential election was his eloquent use of words and expressions. His oratory and uplifting message transformed him almost overnight from underdog to political rock star.

So words can be very powerful. They're never "words, just words." What you stand for—your policies and vision—is inextricably linked to the words you use to communicate it. Obama was inspired by many others as he put together his own voice: a message about change and a delivery style with a spellbinding cadence, particularly with large groups. His voice marked him as a different brand of politician.

Powerful expressions can even take on a life of their own. Look how one of Obama's refrains in his speeches, "Yes, we can," became a viral sensation on the web. Millions viewed the song based on Obama's words after the singer will.i.am (a clever brander himself with that name) and his band the Black Eyed Peas made the catchphrase into a song and posted it on YouTube. The video of the song even went platinum!

Verbal Mastery

The further up the leadership ladder you go, the more important your words—and how you deliver them—become in defining your success. Often policy and vision are crystallized only through the discipline of articulating them with your key advisers. You want to define a clear point of view and style so that your vision and ideas are linked to your words and speaking style, and vice versa, which is what marketers aim for in their ads. And you need to make sure that your voice conveys authority and sounds natural. Every presentation should take people on a journey that persuades them to your way of thinking.

In brand building, your goal is to break through the blur so that people will remember your ideas. Along with naming your ideas and using fresh words and expressions, try to create visual metaphors or images through words and stories. A visual metaphor paints a picture that sticks and even brings numbers and statistics to life. Remember, a vivid visual image can be unforgettable, and stories can be remembered and retold.

Using worn-out words and descriptions will make you seem commonplace. For example, "out-of-the-box thinker" used to be a fresh way of saying "innovative." Now it's so commonplace that when people use it, they seem completely inside the box.

Look at the word *luxury* in the world of brands. Every company in the world that wants the pricing premium of luxury brands has slapped the word *luxury* on its products. The word has become virtually meaningless. It's being used by too many brands that don't provide a "luxury" experience.

The Art of Spontaneous Conversation

You've also got to be ready for spontaneous conversations with both the rank and file and leaders at work. Ever been caught in the elevator with a colleague or even the CEO and found yourself completely dumbstruck? It's happened to me. When you're giving a presentation or speaking at a meeting, you usually at least have an outline prepared in advance, so you have a good idea of what you're going to say.

Impromptu conversations can do wonders for your career because they're personal and may lead to deeper connections or at least a favorable impression. So how do you pull it off so that you take advantage of this great opportunity and don't make a complete fool of yourself? Keep up with the news and bring up something topical—a local or national news story (or if you're a sports fan, the hometown team's latest game). Or bring up an important company issue from the corporate website. Avoid partisan politics and controversy. Try to carry on a short conversation about the other person by commenting on a recent talk he gave, an award she received, a trade story, or a recent trip he took. Ask a specific question ("How was your trip to China?") rather than a general question ("How are you doing?"). If you think the VIP doesn't remember you, introduce yourself to her and mention what you do in the company.

Stand and Deliver

We all know that when it comes to things that cause dread, dying on the spot may seem preferable to public speaking. Frankly, I recommend opting for life and mastering the skill of speaking and presenting to an audience.

There are three main pieces that communicate and influence people: your message, your voice, and your body language. Which do you think is most important?

If you said your message, you're wrong by a long shot. Incredibly, your voice and body language are *more important* than the message. The message you communicate with your voice and the way you stand and move can support or derail your ideas. Yet most of us spend all our time on the message, not the delivery. We need to reverse it.

❋ ❋ ❋

How *you say it trumps* what *you say.*

❋ ❋ ❋

Researchers have even tried to quantify the importance of each. According to one authority, when we are deciding whether we like the person delivering a message, tone of voice accounts for 38 percent, body language 55 percent, and the actual message only 7 percent. It's known as the 7%–38%–55% Rule, or the 3 Vs (for verbal, vocal, and visual).

Replay the Videotape

The secret behind the incredible performances of the TED talk speakers is repeated practice and rehearsal with TED professionals to work on developing a powerful message and delivery. While few of us will have that level of coaching, you can work on your presentation style by videotaping an actual talk or mock presentation and writing down your observations on these points:

- Reflect on how you appear based on what you see and hear. Write down the adjectives that come to mind. What are the key message points you wanted to convey? How could you improve the message and your delivery?

- Ask others to look at the tape and give you feedback. What adjectives come to mind? What are the overall message points that they remember? How could you improve your delivery?

- Turn off the sound and look at the video again. What nonverbal messages do your body stance, stage movements, and facial expressions convey? Write down comments about your posture, gestures, eye contact, animation, and interaction.

- Listen to the audio portion of the video with no picture. Listening to your voice, what adjectives come to mind? Do you change your pitch, volume, inflection, and speed to make your talk interesting? What parts should you emphasize more? How?

Perfect Pitch

Our voice brands us as male or female, as high-class or lowbrow, as American-born or immigrant, as leader or follower. Studies show that an attractive voice increases perceptions of your attractiveness. So if you have a lovely voice, keep talking!

An unforgettably sexy voice can linger through the decades ("Happy birthday, Mr. President"). But women's voices may be a disadvantage. That's because pitch depends on the size of your voice box, and a bigger voice box means a deeper voice. That's powerful, because a deeper voice suggests leadership and authority. It gives the speaker instant credibility. High voices sound unpleasant, while low voices express power. Of course, this works in favor of men.

A whispery, whiny voice or an affectless, low-energy style makes a woman appear weak in an instant and makes it difficult to grab attention at a meeting or in a casual conversation. The high-pitched voice that some women have may be a problem since it is associated with nervousness and excitability. On the other hand, a rough, scratchy sound could make a woman seem more like a man.

Have you ever met someone whose voice seemed to contradict her appearance? The best voice for each of us is our natural voice—not too high and not too low. Listen to your voice on a recorder. How does it sound? Is it too high? Too soft? Too loud? Good speakers vary their pitch and inflection as they make their points. Changes in speed, volume, and pitch keep people engaged in your message.

✳ ✳ ✳

Varying rhythm, volume, and pitch
gets people's attention.

✳ ✳ ✳

Leave yourself a voice mail message, one that you are planning to leave for a colleague. How would you rate your message on clarity, brevity, authoritativeness, and emotional connection?

Engage Your Audience

Confident communicators often begin with banter rather than jumping right into the meat of the message. Banter softens up the audience with something lighthearted. It signals openness and invites the audience to go on a journey with you.

Good speakers have a conversation with the audience. That means greeting people with a smile and making eye contact throughout. You want to convey confidence, energy, and openness but also *interest* in the people you are with. You want people to feel it's really about them. Move around and use your face and arms to express what you are saying. If you are saying one thing but your body is screaming something else, people won't hear your words. Remember the visual!

You're aiming to be a charismatic speaker who gets the audience aroused. Psychologists use the term *arousal* to refer to the degree of audience interest and engagement with what you're saying. The more arousal you generate in your audience, the more appealing you will be as a speaker. Your mantra in developing your talk should be "short, funny, and memorable." In terms of delivery, planting also helps: planting your eyes on key individuals in the audience, and planting your feet on the stage as you move around so that you take ownership of the space.

Since most women are great at reading faces and body language, clue in to when your audience is riveted and when they are losing interest. You may catch people shifting in their chairs, or someone glancing at a watch. When people stop taking notes, that's a clear signal that no one cares anymore. Don't wait until the audience is snoring. Read the clues!

Ten Tips for Great Communicators

Here are ten tips for performing well in presentations and meetings:

1. **Begin and end strong.** Find a way to dramatize your main point at the beginning with a clever visual or phrase, and then reinforce the theme again at the end.

2. **Be creative with your key ideas.** Explore rhetorical devices such as chiasma, which is a play on words that inverts their order in two parallel phrases. Think of John F. Kennedy's famous line, "Let us not negotiate out of fear, but let us never fear to negotiate."

3. **Rehearse exactly as you plan to deliver a talk.** Don't just read your notes or the slides and say, "Next, I'm going to talk about," and think you've rehearsed. You must practice and rehearse as if it is your actual performance with all the stage movement, gestures, pauses, and emphasis you plan to use.

4. **Click with the audience.** A powerful way to click is to be open and reveal something personal. Harvard professor Amy

Cuddy's TED talk on nonverbal communication has been viewed by more than ten million people and in the most riveting portion, Cuddy shares the feelings she had early in her career of "I don't belong here."

5. Lock in your ideas with a memorable name. Chip and Dan Heath, in their book *Made to Stick*, used the acronym SUCCESs to lock in their hook for communicating well: Simple Unexpected Concrete Credentialed Emotional Stories.

6. Be a human, not an expert. As a presenter, you need to convey warmth, energy, and your humanity. Lively anecdotes, stories, and humor will make an audience, even a corporate one, like you.

7. Dance. Think choreography, and move out from behind the podium. Use a wide gesture with both hands for a major point and lean in toward the audience.

8. Sing. Change your voice level and the way you present information: shuffle between loud and low for some points. Vary your pitch and volume. Switch the speed at which you speak, too. Slow down to emphasize the important points. Ask questions. Tell stories. Make points. Cite facts. Mix it up. Pause.

9. Create your own slides. Abandon the common templates—instead look for dramatic visuals and limit yourself to about ten words per slide. You want the star of your show to be you, not wordy slides that everyone will be struggling to read.

10. Become a business storyteller. As a leader, you want to build a narrative around your vision and goals, and tell stories that sell your vision, your business, your products, and yourself. Try to tell stories that people can see as if you were filming a movie

The Most Important (and Most Difficult) Pitch

With all our verbal excellence, we're very good at advocating for others, but we women are notoriously bad at pitching ourselves for a raise, a promotion, or a new job. On Wall Street, a very senior executive told me that the guys come around months before their reviews to lobby for their bonuses. They make their case, even dropping the specific bonus number they think they deserve.

"No women come by to lobby," he said, "and that's a mistake. Because when you are tallying who gets what, you can't help but be influenced. You think, if I don't give him close to what he wants, I may lose him. On the other hand, she never made a request, so maybe I can save some money there."

Being afraid to pitch ourselves and ask for more money is something we must overcome if we want pay parity. Even Mika Brzezinski, cohost of MSNBC's *Morning Joe*, had trouble asking for a raise because she was afraid her bosses would think she was being difficult. In reality, she was looking for fairness because her cohost was making many multiples of her salary. Finally she got serious and laid out her case in a calm not shrill manner.

In negotiating something as emotionally charged as your salary, it pays to be calm, confident and matter of fact. If you get push-back on what you want, tick off the challenging projects you spearheaded, the revenue you brought in, and your other accomplishments. Ask questions to see if you can suggest alternatives so the negotiation is a win-win.

In one of my first jobs in branding, I was having lunch with Dan, a new hire who was at a lower level, and almost choked on my salad when he told me what he was making. After a sleepless night, I summoned the courage to approach our mutual boss. Rather than run in and strangle him, which is what I wanted to do, I decided to try to find common ground and said to him, "I know as a father with four daughters you must be concerned about making sure that women are paid fairly." It worked. In reality, I hadn't negotiated my salary when I interviewed. Like many women, I accepted the offer rather than negotiate for more as Dan had done. It was a mistake that I never made again.

When It's Awkward

Communicating a message that we don't want to deliver and the other person doesn't want to hear makes for a difficult conversation.

Many HR professionals have told me that women have more trouble with difficult conversations than men. Not than anyone likes difficult conversations. The vast majority of managers say they have trouble giving a negative performance review to an employee. But it's particularly hard for women because we don't like conflict and many of us don't want to be perceived as mean.

So how do you master the art of difficult conversations?

We all have to have them. We have to give a poor review to an underperforming employee, or let someone go during a company downsizing. Or, as happened to me, you have to tell the boss about a major screwup. The trick is to deliver the message honestly and fully—and end up with a more or less positive outcome.

As much as you might prefer to delay the meeting or do it over the phone, difficult conversations are best done in person and always privately. Things only get worse when you delay, because then the conversation revolves around, "Why didn't you talk with me sooner?"

Four Tips for Difficult Conversations

Here are some points on mastering difficult conversations:

- **Compose a clear-cut message.** Have in mind the clear, complete message that you need to give to the other person and know how you plan to say it, since it will be remembered and repeated. Don't just tell someone that the way he is handling a project is wrong. Tell him *why*. It doesn't help to hear, " No, I don't like it" or "That won't work." (A good rule of thumb is to never begin a sentence with "No.")

- **Defuse the bomb.** It's going to be a difficult conversation, so defuse that problem by saying so at the beginning: "This is a tough conversation for me. . . ." That should help set a positive tone.

- **Empathize.** Great communicators have the ability to deliver bad news in a way that makes the other person feel understood and not marginalized. A caring demeanor and eye contact are important. You might bring up a personal experience with a similar challenge and how you dealt with it.

- **Let anger fall like water off a duck.** If the other person blows up, let her vent with this image in your mind. Resist yelling back or being intimidated. Keep thinking of water rolling off a duck. That way you'll remain calm and get the conversation back on track when the verbal tirade is over.

E-mail: Beware!

I sent a prospecting e-mail to "Sally," a woman executive I didn't know very well. I wrote the e-mail in a somewhat chatty style since we had worked together some years back.

Now, when you are making a business pitch, a lot of your effort comes to naught or takes a while to develop into something. But because I had known her casually at a previous job, I wasn't prepared for her curt, one-sentence e-mail reply. It stopped me in my tracks as I read it. It sounded so strident and impersonal. I got a totally different impression about her.

And it's not surprising. New neuroscience research is showing that communicating by computer is an emotional wasteland. In contrast, in-person communication is rich in content, nuance, and emotion. That's why e-mail increases the likelihood of misunderstanding.

✸ ✸ ✸

E-mail is often misunderstood because you're communicating in an "emotional wasteland."

✸ ✸ ✸

E-mail is something we dash off quickly, so it's easy to lose touch with how we're coming across. It's easy to forget how something we're writing might come back to bite us. Think three times before clicking on "send."

E-mail can have a long life, as many people have regretfully discovered. E-mails can be dredged up in dismissals and lawsuits, overturning your promising career. So be careful not to send anything that might come back to haunt you, like this e-mail from a top corporate executive to one of her employees, which was sensationalized in the business news: "I think about us together all the time. Little moments like watching your face when you kiss me."

Email and texting are revolutionizing how we communicate, leading to a style of communication that is shorter and more visual. Using *emoji* or other images along with words in texts and e-mails can engage, amuse and persuade. When you overuse them it can appear too cutesy or over the top, just like exclamatory excess!!!

Craft Your Voice Mail

With voice mail, people can't see you, either, but they can hear your voice, which is a very powerful branding mechanism. Think of how quickly you can identify a friend just by hearing a word or two or recognize a celebrity doing a voice-over in a TV commercial or animated movie.

Take a moment to put yourself in a confident, positive state of mind before you speak. Put a smile on your face as you leave the message. It will make a big difference in how you are perceived. Above all, keep voice mail messages short and to the point. There's nothing more annoying than a rambling message that you have to listen to for five minutes, a misstep women seem to make more often than men. So resist the temptation to go into a lot of detail explaining the whys and wherefores. For example, a good message might be, "Sidney, I hope you can attend the meeting on the X project next Thursday. I'm going to recommend a new vendor, and I know you were dissatisfied with the last company as well. With your support, I'm confident we can get the project back on track."

If you're ambitious and want to take your brand somewhere in the world, communicating and speaking well are skills you'll need to master. The higher you go, the more you will be asked to speak at industry meetings or give presentations to the executive committee or the board.

And when your way of communicating clicks, you'll know it. There will be that wonderful moment in a meeting when you feel at one with the audience. You know it when you're connecting—both the content of your message and your way of delivering it are breaking through. You're looking at them. Some are smiling; others are signaling that they have a question. You can feel the energy in the room.

That's when you'll know what it feels like to be a powerful communicator. That's when you'll know it was worth the effort to develop your verbal edge.

A BIGGER VOICE

Carol Ross
executive coach

"Don't get too big for your britches" is an axiom many of us heard while we were growing up. I think it's especially used by immigrant parents like mine who had one foot forever planted in Asia and one tentative foot (or big toe) cautiously testing the waters of a new world. It's a strange expression. But it was planted in my brain early and is still echoing in there today.

Later, I was delightfully surprised when I found a letter to my older sister from my father (who died when I was thirteen) in which he wrote, "Carol is sticking out like a sore thumb. She got the highest grade point average in her class." He was proud of me! I guess he just never told me so that my britches would always fit.

Being a female engineer is sort of like sticking out like a sore thumb, too. And that's how my career started—working for technology companies. My passion, I soon realized, was to be found on the human side of the workplace. My interest started quite selfishly, really. Some of the technology colleagues I valued were thinking of leaving the company, and I didn't want that. I decided to get involved in the company organization and created a new position for myself around retention. I started programs, like a bag lunch series, so that people could discuss their needs and ideas. I was empowering people, and I loved it.

My career now as an executive coach is focused on creating what I call "a bigger voice" for both my clients and myself. It's what we should all strive for. It's not about ego or conquest, which may be the old model. It's more about feminine virtues like helping people and building community. And community is more important than people realize. It has a bottom-line impact on your business. A thriving community will keep your business going through market changes, and you'll be able to harness the ideas and insights of your community.

Here's an example. My husband's music teacher, Ms. Chen, didn't just teach the piano; she created a community, and that community was there recently when she celebrated her sixty-fifth birthday. Former students came from far and wide to be with her. Some hadn't studied with her for twenty years. Some were now far flung and had to travel by plane. One woman drove from Boise to Salt Lake City to pick up another person, and then drove on to Denver for the celebration. Neither rain nor sleet nor long distances will stop people when you have that "bigger voice" and have created a community around your wisdom.

The path to a bigger voice is using your wisdom to build a vibrant community, to create with others. But how do you do that? What's the right mix of technology for reaching your audience and creating a dialogue? How do you create a brand that makes your wisdom easy to hear and understand? How do you develop new relationships and nurture those connections to broaden your reach? How do you create a community that has a life of its own, feeding on a diversity of viewpoints and resulting in collective wisdom?

Many people have a great network inside their company and nothing outside. The company becomes their world. But that's too limiting. It's a big world out there, and we need to think of the world as our network. So much of what holds us back is made up in our heads about who we can approach and who we can't. What's our biggest fear? It's fear of rejection. I want to teach people that when they are able to connect in a genuine way, without wanting something in return, they open the door to receiving the best that people have to offer. It's a paradox, isn't it?

I feel like I've been on the hero's journey of discovery. What I ache to share is the combination of being bold and compassionate, being analytical and intuitive at the same moment. We need to encompass the masculine and feminine worlds in the same breath. That's what I've tried to do using my engineering mind to understand the world and a compassionate heart to see what people yearn for.

My journey is a quest to help people create from their voice a bigger voice.

Women who brand, like commercial advertisers, tap into the power of story to make business messages relevant, memorable, and fun.

5

USE THE POWER OF STORY IN PERSON AND ONLINE

A powerful way to use your verbal edge is through the power of story. Our stories tell people who we are. When you're close to people, you know their story. And you want to make sure people know *your* story, whether you are an executive, an entrepreneur, a lawyer, an interior designer, or an artist.

A story provides meaning to the facts and experiences of your life. It tells people how you want to be remembered. And story is an effective technique for branding, because the human brain remembers things better when they are presented in a narrative rather than in a list or statement. That's why marketers develop brand stories that wrap myth and narrative around their brands. You could look at commercials as mini-movies or brand stories.

It's the same with people. Telling your story doesn't mean telling everything you've ever done. It means crafting a short elevator speech— a thirty-second personal commercial that defines who you are in a way that's interesting, conversational, and different. It means developing a story line when you talk about projects in meetings or accomplishments in interviews so that what you say is memorable. (If people can't remember your story, it has no value.)

An elevator speech is something you will use throughout your life to communicate your personal identity. You'll use it when meeting new people, pitching your idea, or trying to persuade people to choose you for a different, interesting position at your company and, of course, in job interviews.

＊   ＊   ＊

*Your elevator speech:
a thirty-second personal commercial.*

＊   ＊   ＊

Never is an elevator speech more necessary than when you're branding yourself for a career transition. But in reality, every encounter is a potential interview that can lead to an opportunity for you. Yet most of us are unprepared, and we botch the opportunity to make a strong first impression by communicating an arresting brand identity. Many of us spend more time planning our grocery shopping than how we're going to pitch ourselves. As a result, we don't make meaningful connections and don't create demand for our brand.

Most of us don't fully use our linguistic advantages as women when we're trying to promote ourselves. And knowing how to talk about yourself—who you are and what's special about you and your experiences—is critical to success, whether it's branding yourself in the job market, lobbying for a promotion, or selling to clients.

Use Your Elevator Speech to Tell a Story

Recently, I was at a speed-networking event for women. The crowd ranged from new grads and MBAs to mid-level and seasoned executives. It included people in transition, those stuck in jobs they had outgrown, and women looking to reinvent themselves in some way. Some were executives, some entrepreneurs, some lawyers, some academics, and some nonprofit professionals. Each person had sixty seconds to give her elevator speech.

One after the other, the women recited a list of what they had done—schools, job titles, dates of employment, how many people they managed, what the company was about—often in chronological order. It came across like a shopping list.

＊　＊　＊

There's no brand story *in a shopping list.*

＊　＊　＊

Most of the women either didn't have a memorable pitch for selling themselves or didn't have time to get it in before their short time in the spotlight was up. Now, I know men can also be bad at giving elevator speeches, but women have more difficulty in promoting themselves and touting their accomplishments.

For many women, *brag* is a four-letter word, and that's not good because you need to learn how to toot your own horn. Seeking recognition is necessary and positive; if you don't do it, you'll be passed by. It's how you do it that can get you into trouble. You don't want it to come across as obvious self-promotion. The key to effective self-promotion, just as in the best creative writing, is to show, not tell, and the best way to show is to tap into story and the verbal aptitudes women are hardwired for.

Have a Positive Takeaway Message

Before you start to craft your personal commercial or elevator speech, figure out the message you want people to take away from your story. The takeaway message, the core idea or overriding message you want people to take away about you, is your meta-narrative—the master or grand narrative—the story behind the story. It is the overriding idea that all your stories are developed from, and it should be a compelling identity, idea, or message.

For example, no one is interested in messages like "I'm in transition and looking for a job" or "I'm not happy in my current job and I'm looking for something better" or "I've got a business that is going nowhere." No boss is interested in the meta-narrative "frustrated and unhappy employee."

Yet, amazingly, those are the meta-narratives most people dish out when they tell their stories. For example, in the speed-networking event I attended, many women in transition began their elevator speeches with something like "I'm in transition and looking for a job. My last job was . . ." And they tortured us with a very frustrating and unhappy sequence of events. Just seconds into their talks, people were tuning out. That's because the takeaway message was "out of work" and "hapless job-seeker." No one wants to hear that message, even if it is packaged in an interesting story. People want to hear positive messages that captivate them in some way, that give them hope about the person and hold out promise for the future.

Here's a sample Elevator Speech that tells a story about a job accomplishment:

> I think of myself as someone who inhabits the new frontier in digital marketing. Recently, I led the launch of a new consumer electronics product called X. We had a miniscule promotion budget—an amount that wouldn't even have gotten us one TV commercial. So we did low-cost videos for YouTube and a social networking campaign on Facebook. To keep costs down, we shot the first video outside a local high school. Things weren't going well. But then a high school student who was an extra had an extraordinary idea, and things started to click and happen spontaneously on the video. We posted the video on YouTube. My client was thrilled when it went viral, getting us tens of thousands of viewers in a matter of weeks. Of course, digital marketing is new territory, and I don't expect every marketing effort to take off like that, but it's exciting working on the cutting edge of viral marketing. That's where I want to make my mark.

Build Your Story

After you have decided on your meta-narrative or takeaway message, you need to sit down and figure out how to convey the message in a story. Metaphor and analogy are great devices for leading into your story. In describing myself, I sometimes say, "I'm a cross between a brand manager and a business coach." And I might add, "Unlike other business coaches, I'm a personal brand strategist with a background in branding. I use the principles and strategies from the commercial world of brands and apply them to people."

Then I might segue into a client story that brings everything to life. For example, I recently met someone who was trying to switch careers and was having trouble getting anyone in the new field to meet with her. So I told her a story about a Chinese American woman, "Ophelia," who wanted to switch from being a banker to working for a Western luxury-goods manufacturer that was expanding its business in China. By telling Ophelia's story, I conveyed my meta-narrative as a personal brand strategist who used branding principles in an innovative way with clients. And because I did it through story, it was more memorable than a straightforward statement of capabilities.

Disguise Your Message

No one is interested in receiving a job pitch. Just as no one is interested in receiving an advertising message. Or a sales pitch. We're all bombarded with enough unwanted messages daily!

That's why it's smart to study the branding and advertising model. In advertising, product messages are disguised as brand stories in the form of commercials, YouTube videos, profiles on social networking sites, interactive games, events, or product placement on a television show. The job of the creative team is to come up with advertising and marketing ideas that are on strategy, in other words, that convey the agreed-upon takeaway message. The best brand stories often contain very few facts; rather, they convey an entertaining, informative, or humorous "story" that connects with people.

Advertisers select the stories that show their brand in the best light. They obviously don't emphasize deficiencies but instead focus on the areas where their brand shines. And, of course, they may tell stories that highlight the deficiencies of competitive brands. The brand story doesn't even have to be about the product. It can be about its brand audience, their lifestyle and cachet.

✹ ✹ ✹

You're not bragging.
You're telling a story.

✹ ✹ ✹

Stories are powerful for people, too. As in advertising, your story not only can create visual and verbal connections but also can connect emotionally with others. Good stories engage people. A great story, like a great movie, lingers in the consciousness of the people you tell it to and even transforms the way they see you and the larger world. Stories are also powerful because telling stories doesn't look like bragging. You're *telling a story* about yourself, a demanding client, a team you led, a tough assignment that had a lot of moving parts, a recent meeting, whatever.

Men Are from LinkedIn, Women Are from Facebook

Don't neglect to take your personal branding skills and storytelling skills to the Internet. When you look at the stats, you see similar preferences and ways of communicating played out in the digital world that we see in the offline world. For men, an important goal of communication is conferring status and power while women seek consensus and community.

Look at social media. A lot of attention has been focused on women being more active online than men. It's true that, worldwide, women spend more hours per week on social media, but we tend to use social media for staying in touch with family and friends on sites like Facebook and on photo-sharing sites like Pinterest.

So while women "do digital," we don't use social media as a personal branding and networking tool the way men do. Women are very connected with a small, tight group online in contrast to men, who are more active in the networking and career-enhancing potential of business sites like LinkedIn. Rather than using social media to connect with family and friends, men use social sites to show status and to share accomplishments. They're also more active in the blogosphere promoting their opinions, trends observed in a number of studies on social media and gender.

Look at Twitter, a site that is popular with both men and women, yet men are much more likely to post their own tweets, while women are more likely to use Twitter as a conversation medium and to follow people they admire. It's a missed opportunity.

Tell Your Story Well Virtually

One of the best ways to invest in your brand is to take the time to craft a strong profile on LinkedIn. The best profiles tell a story, a career story, that ties all the pieces of your journey together into a coherent whole that's compelling and unusual.

Realize that a weak digital imprint is like a weak reputation. People won't think you're as good as people who have a strong presence on the Internet. Everyone is going to Google you anyway, so it's important to take charge of your brand virtually to tell your career story.

From a business branding perspective, LinkedIn should be your first stop on the social media express. It's the number one business site, actively used by HR professionals, recruiters, and businesspeople. Yet, more men than women use LinkedIn and men are more active in linking up with business colleagues.

* * *

Think of LinkedIn as your narrative bio, résumé, cover letter, recommendations, and business head shot all aggregated in one place, where it will be looked at repeatedly.

* * *

Profiles with a captivating narrative flow are sticky; they're easy to remember. Weave in key projects, successes, credentials, and turning points in your career. Ditch aspects of your journey that take people off course for your brand, unless you can make them part of your story (missed flight leads to new business opportunity). Avoid insider jargon, so that who you are and the value you offer are understandable to a broad audience.

The three most important elements on a LinkedIn profile are the headline, career summary, and photo. These are what people view first, like the front page, above-the-fold stories in a newspaper.

The LinkedIn headline is like an ad headline so take the time to craft a headline that conveys your value and defines who you are professionally in a brief but compelling way. (The LinkedIn headline is about the same length as a tweet so it will take a little finesse to say a lot in a few words.)

For the LinkedIn career summary, write a career narrative that conveys your brand identity and the distinct, relevant value you bring, highlighting major accomplishments, awards, and the like. Try to use all the keywords and buzzwords that people might use to search for someone like you, and update your profile regularly to put in new skills, accomplishments, and current buzzwords. The LinkedIn profile also includes sections where you can highlight your detailed job history, awards, publications, and links to your website or blog. There are also special services for which you can pay extra and have your profile featured on searches.

Learn the Art of Storytelling

If you're worried about your ability to talk about yourself and your accomplishments in a narrative way, look at the key elements that have characterized storytelling through the centuries:

> **Heroine.** You'll need a *likable* protagonist (that's you). Being a likable but flawed heroine is even better! Think of your audience and how you can best portray the aspects of your story so that your audience will identify with you and your experiences.
>
> **The MacGuffin.** A term coined by Alfred Hitchcock, the MacGuffin is the catalyst that sets and keeps everything in motion and compels you to take action. In Hitchcock's *North by Northwest*, the MacGuffin is the microfilm of government secrets that the men chasing Cary Grant want to get their hands on. Your MacGuffin could be a global project with a tight deadline that you were assigned after the last manager flubbed it.
>
> **Trials and Difficulties.** In theater, the obstacles, frustration, and conflict the heroine has to deal with are introduced in the second act. Likewise, you'll want to talk about your experience on a specific project, bringing to life the conflicts and challenges you faced. Use dialogue to bring the story to life. ("Then, at 11 P.M., my client called to tell me. . . .")
>
> **The Turning Point.** All good stories have a turning point. The obstacles seem insurmountable, and then—poof!—the heroine (you) perseveres and succeeds against all odds. In plays, this typically is the cliffhanger that ends the second act. Sometimes the turning point is psychological, a change in attitude, not necessar-

ily a cataclysmic event. It can be something that you don't recognize as the real tipping point until later.

Resolution. This is the final act, when we find out what happens and the story ends happily or tragically. Of course, since you're selecting the story, share one with a successful ending, particularly if you are marketing yourself. Or, if everything doesn't work out perfectly at the end of your story, there should be an important lesson that you learned. (I remember my mom's words, "When you fail, at least learn something from it.")

Embrace the Struggle

As a woman, you shouldn't have any difficulty coming up with examples of your personal career struggles. But emphasizing the difficult journey, even embracing your failures, is smart storytelling and smart branding, too. Americans love nothing as much as stories about individuals who struggled and came out wiser and stronger in the end. Even stories about projects or jobs with bad endings are poignant and powerful, since we also love redemption stories.

There seems to be some difference between the way women and men tell a story. Men tend to emphasize their command of a situation as they overcome obstacles, while women often have a more organic approach, emphasizing the role of others and leaving room for a degree of luck and serendipity, with one thing leading to another. Both ways can be fun.

✹ ✹ ✹

Emphasize the journey,
not your "victory."

✹ ✹ ✹

Stories that reveal your shortcomings and mistakes are always great to share when you're rallying your team, speaking at an industry event, or trying to talk about yourself in a self-deprecating way, such as when you're giving a keynote address. The audience will love you because you're showing you're human, just like them. And it's much more attractive than just talking about how successful you or your company has been.

One of the reasons stories are so powerful is that they are a concise and memorable way of telling a complex history or series of events. The best stories contain a meaning or moral that isn't explicitly stated so that the listener has to *participate* in filling in the missing pieces. Good stories don't define. They *reveal* meaning.

The best stories reflect deep cultural themes: atonement, redemption, and the struggle for advancement. Here are some tried-and-true core themes that can help you develop your story:

- **The Hero's Journey.** Hero stories, like that of Ulysses, feature a hero who goes out in the world and accomplishes great things. You're a hero, too, when you take on a difficult assignment and succeed.

- **Creation.** Creation stories focus on how you became who you are or how you started your business.

- **Transformation.** Transformation narratives contain a defining moment that changed your career or life.

- **Redemption.** Redemption is an age-old and deeply American theme. Your story could be about your conflict with personal demons or how you fell from grace and then found your way back.

- **Crossroads.** Crossroads stories feature an important juncture where you had to choose between X and Y, the rationale behind your decision, and the impact on your life.

You can also look at female archetypes for ideas on how to position yourself as a protagonist: heroine, female leader, wise woman, explorer, earth mother, or artist.

Learn from Master Storytellers

Recently I gave a talk at a women's convention where the keynote speaker was the historian Doris Kearns Goodwin, an expert storyteller. Now, presidential history can be a pretty elite topic, but Goodwin made it relevant and riveting for the women in the room by telling a series of stories.

Her first story recounted how she became a historian because of baseball. She was a Brooklyn Dodgers fan as a young girl, and one of her "jobs" was to recount each day's ball game to her father when he came home from work. At first, when her dad came home, she blurted out, "The Dodgers won today!" But she learned that when she built up the excitement play by play, she had her dad hanging on her every word, and that's how she became a storyteller and a historian.

Then Goodwin told a series of stories about working with Lyndon Johnson. One day, for example, President Johnson told her that he wanted to meet with her personally, and Goodwin was worried. Johnson had a minor-league reputation as a womanizer. "What was going to happen?" she wondered. Goodwin built the suspense, finally telling us that Johnson's first words were "You remind me of my mother," which brought down the house.

Invite Them In

Goodwin also talked about the conflict she faced as a historian at Harvard University and a mother with three boys. While many of us in the audience might not identify with hanging out with a president or being tenured faculty at Harvard, we could all identify with the dual roles and push-pull between our work, our homes, and ourselves.

After she left Harvard, Goodwin began work on her book about Franklin Delano Roosevelt and his wife, Eleanor, and she told us how she was elevated by the life story of Eleanor Roosevelt (particularly since she felt her own identity had been diminished after leaving Harvard). She regaled us with many interesting stories, including one about Eleanor lobbying her husband to make one allowance for the nonmilitary use of rubber during World War II, the manufacture of women's girdles! And how, at all of her press conferences, she allowed only women journalists. (Since this was a women's conference, that point really hit home.)

Near the end of her talk, Goodwin spoke about Abraham Lincoln, the subject of another book, and how humor and storytelling were key factors in his political success. She told stories about Lincoln's many setbacks and early concern that he would die and have contributed nothing to the world and, most important to him, have done nothing to be remembered by. Goodwin had a moving end to her talk, coming full circle to baseball and going to the Boston Red Sox games with her own family today.

Craft Your Screenplay

When I was a kid, Mom sometimes asked me, "Is that the truth, or are you telling a story?" In those days, "telling a story" meant you were making something up. When I talk about portraying your brand for marketing yourself, I mean using the facts. Of course, it's your interpretation of the facts.

Good branding is always built on authenticity. But no one said you have to use all the facts! You're framing your story so that you maximize your assets and make it interesting to other people. This is an important message, because most women underplay their assets, and it's time for that to change.

All good branding involves sacrifice. You have to focus your brand around one compelling idea, not three or four. And it's the same with you and your personal story. Good stories undergo good editing. You need to leave parts out that will take people in the wrong direction. (Go back to your meta-narrative idea.) Too much information is deadly. Leave out things that are not important or conflict with your core message. Going off on tangents (my specialty) is confusing. You want to have a narrative thread that shows consistent values, motivations, and a sense of self, even if you have made radical career switches.

This doesn't mean your story should be static. We are always updating our treatment of our own lives. And the narrative I use this year is very different from my stories of five years ago. The story I tell to a corporate audience is different from the ones I tell to students or entrepreneurs or a group of all-women executives.

I'm telling a true story, but I'm telling the story that's right for them.

Keep It Positive

The way you replay specific memories shapes your life story, even shapes your destiny. That's why articulating your life and career in a drama is not just memorable branding. It will also help you understand who you are and will be.

There is a strong connection between the stories people tell and their actual life experience. The way we visualize and tell our life stories has a profound impact on how we think about ourselves, how we act, and even whether we succeed. The narratives we tell shape our experiences, so make them positive and authentic but try not to sell yourself short.

More women than men have impostor syndrome, especially the high-achieving women. It's the feeling that you're not good enough and people are going to find you out. We all get this feeling from time to time—that's normal. But many talented women make a habit of this kind of negative thinking. Even when they do well, they think they performed badly. In self-assessments, more men think they'll do well and rate themselves highly afterward. Studies show that men are more comfortable bluffing, or if they know 50 percent of an answer, they'll raise their hands and fake the rest. Many women won't volunteer unless they are completely sure they know the answer.

Changing the way we see ourselves and the stories we tell about ourselves may help us alter our narrative in a more positive direction. Always accentuate the good that came out of something rather than the bad. In studies, people who had sad stories but told them in reverse order, so that the sad story was linked to a good outcome, were more positive and grounded. (For example, say, "I was able to discover an exciting new career for myself as a result of losing that job" rather than "I lost my job but finally I was able to get started in a new career.")

What you don't want to do is tell a happy story marred by a dark detail. ("The job was a great opportunity in a good company, but my boss was demanding and liked to micromanage.") A good way to move beyond painful memories is to think about these experiences in the third person. It will help you reframe and distance yourself from the experience so that you're not stuck there.

✺ ✺ ✺

Don't focus on what went wrong.
Focus on what you learned.

✺ ✺ ✺

In telling our stories, we learn what our experiences meant. If you tell stories about your ability to succeed, you are more likely to succeed in the future. Not that you don't have to take action, too, but it pays to get good at recasting memories so that you see the silver lining, since that will help you reshape your bigger life story.

Good stories have a way of coming true if you focus and act on them long enough.

MATTER AND VOID

Edwina Sandys
sculptor and artist

If you were to ask someone to pick the most recognizable name of the twentieth century, they might well choose my grandfather, Winston Churchill. I believe I've inherited at least some of his traits. Like him, I'm ambitious, sociable, and artistic. Like him and my American great-grandmother, Jennie Jerome, I love America, where I now make my home.

Unlike him, I have never been a smoker, but one of my earliest Proustian memories is the rich, all-pervading smell of his cigars.

I came to be an artist rather late, starting off with the usual women's things like marriage and children. I thought marriage was exciting. I felt grown up and loved being in charge of my own domain. I was happy with my domestic life but also felt the desire for a wider stage. I considered running for Parliament. That was the biggest thing I could think of doing. But my husband was already set to be a member of Parliament, and he and his constituency thought they needed me to work with them full-time to help him get elected. I acquiesced and gave up my parliamentary plans, wrote a novel instead, and then found the muse of painting.

I entered the art world at about age thirty and was showing my paintings at galleries in London and New York. Since my work was selling better here, I began spending more and more time on this side of the Atlantic.

Few artists like promoting themselves. And if you're a woman and English, you can feel even more inhibited. Artists think that if you're good, you'll be recognized, but you need to run it like a business, too. I was brought up like most of us with the old notion that a woman shouldn't pursue anything aggressively. Nobody likes a pushy woman, I always heard. Thankfully, that has changed. I remember when I was hiring a housekeeper once, and she quoted me a very high rate. "Isn't that quite high?" I asked. She replied, "Well, I'm the best." Quite right. That's not pushy—that's smart.

An artist often needs to be assertive to get that commission. And the clients expect you to be. They need to be reassured. "That sculpture will be magical in front of your building, and I'd love to create it for you."

In my art, I've been exploring the positive and the void, the yin and yang, the two sides of the brain. I look for subjects that have the in and out, where the empty spaces are important, too. What we don't say and see is as important as what we do. The space you leave empty is as important as the space you fill. In my art, I look for themes that portray this drama. Part of the challenge is taking away everything that is not relevant to what I am portraying. Michelangelo said it best when asked how he created David out of a block of marble. He said, ˜I just removed everything that wasn't David."

Exploring both sides is necessary to develop yourself fully. If you have children and they are artistic, don't just have them study artistic things. Have them also go into the other side of the brain and do something like mathematics. Toggle back and forth. When you create something, you go into a trance artistically, but as you develop it, you bring in the logical part of yourself. Then, you readjust it and let it fly again. To be successful today, we need to align our artistic and logical sides or have a partner who can fill the void.

As an artist, I want to create work that stops people in their tracks. I want people to look at an artwork as something for them to consider, something to look at, something that will have a lingering effect and keep coming back in their memories. I want them to think how the world is a little different from the way they thought it was before.

I want my work to stay with them.

Women who brand realize that
what you build in other people's minds through images
has a way of coming true. A power pose makes a
power brand.

6
VISUAL ASPECTS OF APPEARANCE AND POWER

Should attractiveness matter? In an ideal world, probably not.

But it's not an ideal world, and we're just kidding ourselves if we deny that attractiveness is a factor in success. It won't help if you feel that the world of surfaces and self-presentation is beneath you. Besides, we can all project attractiveness, and as women, we have more at our disposal to do that. Men wear a "uniform" to work compared to women, who can work with a wide variety of clothes, accessories, hairstyles, and makeup. We have more assets and more opportunities to brand with our image. But because women do not have a recognized fashion code, as men do, we also have more opportunities to make mistakes with our visual presentations.

Make the Most of What You've Got

Women are often victims of the tyrannical idea of natural beauty. Few women think they have it. Case in point, only 4 percent of women around the world consider themselves beautiful according to Dove's "Real Beauty" campaign. In reality, attractiveness is something we can all acquire. Of course, it's easier if you're young, tall, and thin, but it's amazing what a good hairstyle, flattering clothes, and good grooming can do for a gal.

Consider the French. They haven't cornered the market on attractive people. Yet they seem to realize that all women can be attractive. French women understand that attractiveness is about making the most of what you have. And that's a powerful attitude, because attractiveness is a career asset, and everybody can boost her attractiveness.

✹   ✹   ✹

Look good—feel confident—perform better—get paid more.

✹   ✹   ✹

It's the same in the branding world. Branders select packaging and product design that quickly engage a potential customer and appeal to the eye. Of course, you still need a good product under the packaging, just like you need to be good at what you do. But the packaging just makes it more likely that people will realize the product's worth.

You don't need an hourglass figure or perfect facial features to be attractive. Over time, I've made peace with most of my physical flaws. The truth is that I feel better and more confident when I look my best. I find that I'm more articulate, more persuasive, more everything. Even putting on lipstick can be a real pick-me-up. As Mom said, "Put on some lipstick. It'll make you feel better."

Being attractive doesn't mean you have to be drop-dead gorgeous. That can be an impediment, too, since the perception may be that you're not very smart. I've come to admire people who make the most of what they have, rather than the beautiful people, and I think our society does, too. Personal style can transform someone from unattractive into a person to admire and emulate.

First Impressions Are Fast, Lasting, and Visual

We are branded in less than the blink of an eye: Hire–don't hire, strong–weak, like–dislike, attractive–not attractive.

These first impressions are largely visual shortcuts based on how you look and your clothes but also on more subtle visual clues: how you enter the room, how you carry yourself, and your facial expressions. The remarkable thing is that these snap impressions are amazingly accurate and dovetail with the impression we have of someone after knowing him for a long period of time.

Whether we like it or not, it's human nature to appreciate attractiveness and want to trust in our instincts. Even day-old babies react differently to an attractive face. Within the first half second, our eyes lock on the attractive people in a group. And throughout our lives, attractiveness is something we won't be able to resist. Attractive CEOs even have a strong impact on stock price when they first appear on TV.

So, ladies, while we may not like it, image makes a difference in how we are perceived. Our success in the workplace, as in life, is based on creating positive impressions about ourselves. That's why we have to make some effort with our appearance. We ignore it at our peril.

Two prominent economists proved the beauty premium with a research study based on a mock labor market in which students were employers and job seekers. The "job" was solving mazes.

The job seekers wrote out résumés and, as a measure of self-confidence, were asked to estimate how many mazes they could solve in fifteen minutes. Then they were given a simple maze to solve.

Next, the researchers had each employer hire a small number of job applicants. Some employers considered only the résumés of potential employees. Others saw a résumé and a photograph. Some received a résumé and conducted a telephone interview. Others got a résumé, had a telephone interview, and saw a photograph. The last group got the whole nine yards—a résumé, a telephone interview, and an in-person meeting. (A separate group categorized all the job seekers as either attractive or not attractive.)

The good news is that those with good looks were no better than less attractive people at solving mazes. But the startling news was the power of looks. When employers saw a picture or met the job applicant, the beauty premium kicked in. Attractive people got the jobs, were offered bigger salaries, and were expected to be more productive. Attractive people even fared better when there was just a telephone interview, leading researchers to suggest that attractiveness gives people more confidence that is conveyed in their voices and conversation.

✳   ✳   ✳

"Attractive" people are
perceived *as being better.*

✳   ✳   ✳

Both men and women employers had the beauty bias. The bottom line on beauty: attractive men make 4 percent more than similar but average-looking men and the ugliest guys make 13 percent less. One study followed people over decades and found that the attractiveness advantage stays with people over time, even as they age. Like it or not, attractiveness gives you a career boost. And lacking it can derail you or relegate you to the lower echelons of achievement.

The Halo Effect

Self-presentation—your visual identity—is important because of the link people make between what something looks like on the outside and what is on the inside. This attitude has a long history. The ancient Greeks and Romans felt that physical beauty was synonymous with interior beauty.

We do this even today despite all the familiar admonitions, such as "Beauty is only skin deep" or "Don't judge a book by its cover." The fact is, looks have a profound influence on our judgment of a brand or a person.

Good looks also have what social scientists call the *halo effect*. Because something is attractive, we assign many other positive attributes to it that have nothing to do with looks. Attractive people are perceived to be more intelligent, productive, kind, trustworthy, talented, and are even judged more competent leaders and harder negotiators.

Why is that? It may be because the area of the brain that rates looks also rates the goodness of a behavior. So if we think someone is attractive, we make positive assumptions about her mind and heart. The brain wiring that gets confused about "What is beautiful is good" also gets mixed up in the other direction, so we think "What is good is beautiful."

The beauty premium cuts across gender, numerous cultures, and jobs. That's why it's important to pay attention to it and create a look or style that shows you to advantage so that people will have a lot of positive assumptions about you, too—that you're smart, productive, and right for the job. I believe that we can all package ourselves attractively, regardless of natural beauty, age, or weight. Today, having an interesting look or a different personal style is attractive. Besides, being kind and doing nice things for others makes you attractive.

You Have the Tools

Like it or not, from a Darwinian perspective, physical attractiveness and variety in visual presentation are part of the female route to success. Social scientists draw a connection between the importance of looks for women and our greater variety in physical appearance.

The difference in visual presentation between the genders is enormous. Men have it simpler and easier. Career dress is an easily deciphered formula. They could put on a dark suit or khakis and a shirt and wear the same outfit day after day for a month, and no one would even notice as long as they changed the tie or shirt periodically. If a woman wore the same two suits day after day, that would raise eyebrows. In recent years there has been more variety in male dress and accessories, but compared to women, the male-brand image still is more generic.

Variety and distinctiveness give women a branding advantage. We can choose to wear suits, dresses, and pantsuits. We're not limited to the dark blues and black that dominate men's wardrobes. Imagine the eyes that would turn if a man showed up in a lime green or even a maroon suit, yet women can wear practically any color under the sun. We're able to choose bright colors or neutrals, prints or solids, wool or linen, cotton or synthetics.

❋   ❋   ❋

Clothes, hairstyles, accessories, and makeup:
Women have more variety for crafting their visual brand.

❋   ❋   ❋

Most men add a dash of individuality with just a tie or, in a casual workplace, a shirt. But we have our accessories: earrings, necklaces, and bracelets, not to mention handbags and shoes. All these items make us attractive and distinct from other women—more branded. Granted, some men are into stylish clothes, jewelry, or tattoos, but as a rule, most aren't and tend to have a narrower range of clothes, jewelry, shoes, and the like and to own fewer items. The vast difference between the ways men and women approach appearance includes the wide range of hairstyles and makeup women sport compared to men.

Under the Microscope

In our visual age, we've become obsessed with the way things look. And no one gets dissected and scrutinized more than women. When prominent businesspeople and professionals are under the floodlights, it's the women who get the most scrutiny on their looks and appearance.

You can be the CEO of a Fortune 100 company, and, inevitably, if you're a woman, a reporter is bound to ask, "Who designed the suit you're wearing?" In the news story, you'll likely find a description of your clothes, your hair, and your jewelry. And if you're a high-profile woman, be prepared to be examined by scores of media sibyls.

Since we're going to be scrutinized more, why not use it to our advantage? Why not dress to telegraph our brand message? Why not package ourselves as a premium brand? We can dress to inspire and project authority but in a softer more approachable way. Look at Diane Sawyer—she avoids trendiness but looks stylish and strong. She looks appropriate, but not overly cautious as a dresser. She looks like her own woman. She looks like a winner.

For women, there's a double bind with the way we look, so it pays to heed the unwritten style rules we have to learn to be successful in the professional world:

- Be attractive but not glamorous.
- Be feminine but not sexy.
- Be strong but not severe.
- Be stylish but not trendy.

It's not easy, because if we come across as too soft and feminine, people will wonder if we're tough enough for the job, and if we come across as too tailored and masculine, they won't want us in the job because we're too tough.

All these snap judgments happen quickly, in just a fraction of the first second: attractive or unattractive, hire or don't hire, successful or loser. They're based on flash visual impressions: how you look, your clothes, your hair, your posture, even the way you inhabit space.

People won't really hear what you say until they've sized up your visual identity. And we're all guilty of making these snap judgments based on a person's appearance. Social scientists talk about thin-slicing, the ability to see something for a few seconds and form a very accurate impression about it. Incredibly, that blink-of-an-eye impression usually matches the opinion we have after considered analysis. New research shows that we don't even need a full second to grasp something. Just a *microthin* slice—in some studies, just *two-tenths of a second*—is enough time for a person to take something in and evaluate it. So be prepared. (As Mom said, "Half the battle is looking successful.")

Fashion Is Ideas

Taking an interest in clothes can seem frivolous or bourgeois, girly or nonintellectual. Many successful career women I know think that talk of clothes and fashion is beneath them. As someone once said to me, "No thoroughbred was ever a clotheshorse." But you don't have to be an avid reader of *Vogue* or even take an interest in fashion to build a wardrobe that helps you communicate your brand message.

Look at how First Lady Michelle Obama sends messages with her clothes. Her choices of immigrant designers subtly telegraphs multi-culturalism and the quest for the American dream, core themes in the president's speeches. At the inauguration, the new first lady dressed her daughters not in designer duds, but in J. Crew so that they appeared accessible to the average American.

Fashion is a balancing act. You don't want to look like you're obsessed with clothes and neglect your mind. But playing it too safe and proper says that you're insecure and dull. It's all about interpretation.

Perhaps because the pairing of women and power is relatively new, dress may be a danger zone for female executives. Heaven forbid, if you play it too downscale or too sexy, you could be a liability to your company. In fact, two image consultants I know get steady business from corporate executives who don't want to confront female employees with their fashion faux pas and hire consultants to do the dirty work.

Clothes can even make a difference in how well you do the job because they can make you feel attractive and confident, which always helps, particularly in tough situations. The right clothes will have a significant effect on what people think about you on the job. Clothes are a quick read, a symbolic language, one of the easiest ways to communicate information about who you are. In many ancient cultures, clothing was very precise. You could look at people and tell the class they belonged to by the color, style, and motifs of their clothes. In our society today, people judge us by our clothes and how we put ourselves together, just as in those ancient cultures.

Want to Be a Player? Look Like a Player

For most career women, there's one thing you must do with your image. You must project authority.

If you work in a corporate job, you can get ideas on how to project authority with your clothes by looking at what female politicians (think Nancy Pelosi) and news anchors (look at Katie Couric or your local television anchors) wear.

Women in the public eye are under so much surveillance that you can take advantage of the feedback they receive daily. They are good barometers of what works in terms of clothes, hairstyles, and jewelry for women of substance. But you don't want to copy someone. You want to create your own brand look. When Arianna Huffington started appearing on TV, she noticed that all the other women were wearing suits with shirts underneath. "But I thought, 'Why do we all have to look like men?'" Huffington explained, and she opted for something that wasn't a suit. By choosing feminine blouses and dresses, she makes a statement that's feminine yet strong. "I also have a limited color palette," she added. "But this way who you are and what you say can be the focus rather than your red suit or green jacket."

Look also at what successful women in your organization wear. Not that you are going to clone their wardrobes, but if your goal is to rise in the organization, you need to look like someone who could be invited to the executive floor. You might even get a store expert or a personal image consultant to help you put together a look that conveys the brand image to which you aspire and is also distinctive and suited to you. From a branding perspective, you have an opportunity to really make your mark. Find a few designers whose clothes work for you and concentrate on them.

If the dress code in your company is formal attire for the senior executives and casual attire for the rank and file, mix both business casual and formal business attire as your regime. Keep a jacket at the office. Then if an unexpected client meeting comes up, you won't be excluded. But even though so many senior executives never dress down, that doesn't mean things haven't loosened up. Take pantyhose. There's a raging debate in some offices about whether you can toss them in the dustbin and go bare legged, an act that would have caused heads to turn not too long ago. So you have to figure out what's right for the culture where you work.

Accessories can be an area where women have trouble. They either have no accessories or too many for the outfit and occasion. Let me share two secrets a stylist friend told me about. Knowing what to remove is as important as knowing what to add. She always starts with too much then begins the process of elimination until the accessories are just right. You want to aim for a balance between style and restraint.

The other stylist principle is to buy (and wear) only what you love. If you don't love it and feel good in it, pass it up at the store even if it's the bargain of the century. And if you have things that are just okay in your closet, please give them away. In order to perform at your best, it's important to look your best and that means wearing things you love.

Don't be the most casually dressed person in your company. Casual Friday is easy for the guys: it's khakis and a shirt. For ladies, it's a skirt and blouse, a dress, or nice pants. Don't wear jeans, shorts, T-shirts, or flip-flops, except to the company beach party or barbeque, or jogging pants, unless it's the corporate charity run. On the West Coast, where things are more casual, take your cue from what the more senior women are wearing.

Don't Neglect Your Virtual Image

If you have ever marketed yourself on Match.com, you know how important having a flattering picture is to your dating success. It's the same on the Internet and social media sites like LinkedIn. Your picture will be examined more than you realize by recruiters, colleagues, and professional associates of all types. Get a good-quality picture that lets your personality and brilliance shine, not a hastily taken selfie, group shot, or vacation pic. It's important to dress the part for your career and industry, so ditch the glam unless you are in the fashion industry and forgo the casual jeans and T-shirt unless you work at a tech start-up.

Having no picture is not the way to go either. You're seven times more likely to have your profile viewed if you have a picture. Besides, people make the assumption that something is wrong if you don't have a photo. (It's not easy being green.) If someone is trying to look you up after having met you at a business event, your picture makes it easier for people to remember who's who as well.

Be in Sync

A job interview is the time to make sure that the message you're conveying is pitch-perfect. People are making hiring decisions based on little information, so the way you look takes on increased importance. Put as much effort into planning your wardrobe as you do into planning your answers to interview questions. For example, take "Amelia," who wore her best power suit for a job interview at a start-up merchandiser. She clicked with the two young entrepreneurs who had started the enterprise, but she did notice that everyone was casually dressed. For her callback interview, Amelia played it safe by choosing another power suit. But it turned out to be the wrong thing to wear, and the feedback she got when she was dropped from the list of contenders was that the founders felt she was too corporate and wouldn't fit in with a hands-on start-up.

The area that often goes haywire for women is evening events. It's one thing if an administrator wears a plunging neckline to a business event, but if a mid-level or senior woman does it, tongues will wag. You might think you're just being liberated or stylish like the celebrities we see walking the red carpet, but exposed skin sends signals to men that you may not intend. After all, the area of the brain pertaining to sexual pursuit is twice as large in men, and that's not the part of the male brain you want to stimulate at work.

That's You!

A signature accessory or color can be a smart branding device for Brand You. Your trademark could be unusual combinations of jackets and pants. For example, Sarah Palin uses unusual glasses as a branding statement. It could be a fabulous necklace collection that is always part of your wardrobe. Or it could be a color or color palette that you adhere to religiously—brands think of owning a color.

Your business card is part of your visual identity, too, and the company-issue business card is very corporate and generic in appearance. Many women are dumping the corporate cards outside of official business in favor of personal calling cards that are beautiful and distinctive. Your custom-made business card is the perfect thing to use for non-company-related activities and social occasions.

Often these cards are stylishly elegant, with a simple graphic mark or monogram in color and no contact information whatsoever. That way you can write in what you think is appropriate for each person, making it highly individualized. Or you can have the minimum: name, e-mail, and phone (either your direct line or your assistant's). Carry your personal cards in a special card case and have a nice pen—it's all part of your branding. Think about presentation and spend some time on the format of your other business marketing materials, like your résumé. You could add corporate logos in color next to the company names in your job experience list; they would stand out and contribute visual appeal to the document.

Do Something with Your Hair

Hair is a powerful branding device, especially for women. Think of what her stiff helmet hairstyle says about Queen Elizabeth II. Or what Katie Couric's chin-length modern bob says about her. Or the impression you convey if you're stuck in a hairstyle reminiscent of Alice in Wonderland.

It's as if there are hair police who have it out for women. As Dee Dee Myers, the first female presidential press secretary, said, "People don't hear a word you say until they get over your hair." For women, unfortunately, gray hair is aging and could hurt your career. An actress friend with wonderful silver hair asked me if she should color her hair. The problem? She's being cast in roles that call for a sixty-five-year-old woman, and she's only in her early fifties. If she wants younger parts, the answer is yes.

Then again, the decision to color your hair is not a hard and fast rule. Christine Legarde's silver hair is so stylish, it's not aging but a distinctive part of her brand that conveys gravitas and style.

Strike a Power Pose

Ever notice how men tend to spread out and take up a lot of real estate at the conference table while most women sit neatly and compactly? It's a mistake. New research shows posture and the way you sit in a meeting has a big impact on how you are *perceived* and on how you actually *perform*.

Standing tall, leaning in or taking up space at the conference table convey power and leadership to others. Plus there's an added boost. Expansive poses change your body chemistry. They increase testosterone, the dominance hormone, and decrease the stress hormone cortisol, so you feel more confident, composed, and energetic. Crossing your arms, slouching, or taking up a small amount of space communicate low power to others and don't give you the testosterone boost.

You get the power pose advantage whether you do the poses in front of others or by yourself before a meeting or important call, even if you do them just for two minutes, according to a Harvard Business School study.

You probably won't be surprised to hear that men tend to use high-power poses and women tend to take low-power stances. Why not spark feelings of power before important meetings and conversations? Don't hunch over a smartphone or laptop before an important meeting, which automatically puts you into a low-power state of mind. Take a couple of minutes to prepare by striking a power pose so you project power and confidence.

Here are some common high-power and low-power poses.

High-Power Poses:

- Taking a wide stance with hands on hips
- Standing tall and leaning slightly forward with hands at one's side
- Leaning forward over desk with hands planted firmly on the surface
- Walking in toward the group
- Open gesture with hands outstretched
- Spreading out and taking up conference table real estate
- Expansive seated position with arms crossed behind head
- Nodding, smiling face

Low-Power Poses:

- Leaning back or slumping
- Crossed arms in front of chest or crossed legs or ankles in a closed body posture
- Taking up a small amount of space at the conference table
- Walking away from the group
- Flailing arms or too much movement
- Touching the face, neck, or hair too much

A lawyer friend told me that she revs up before entering the courtroom by taking a brisk walk outside (or down the corridor), to get her energy level up, then stands tall and enters the courtroom very slowly and confidently. Interestingly, just improving your posture boosts your self-esteem.

Look Beyond Looks

Attractiveness is a many-faceted thing. It includes appearance, grooming, and personal style, but it goes way beyond your looks. It's hard to find a single measure of attractiveness, and a lot of attractiveness clearly is not facial beauty but being pleasant and looking healthy, relaxed, and fit. So adopting a weekly exercise routine and getting enough sleep can do wonders for your appearance. (Not to mention everything else.)

Personality can make someone a person to admire and emulate. Attractiveness is also your character, your charisma, the sound of your voice, the way you stand and move, the way you write, even your wit and humor. All these things send branding messages. They reflect who you are on the inside.

Attractiveness is also projecting confidence, being comfortable in your own skin. It's in the way you inhabit space, even in how you move. Look at Marilyn Monroe. She's become an icon not just because she was considered beautiful (after rebranding herself by changing her name from Norma Jean Baker and bleaching her hair). Many contemporaries felt that she had the perfect body measurements (37C-23-36, in case you wanted to know), giving her an ideal waist-to-hip ratio (0.64).

Monroe's attractiveness also came from the way she moved. Sure, she had a lovely face and figure, but she paired these assets with a pronounced hip sway or practiced sashay. She was careful to exploit this any time she was "on" as Marilyn. If she had moved with a lumbering gait or been awkward, she wouldn't have appeared beautiful.

Mild Flirtation vs. Being Flirtatious

Ever since Adam and Eve, putting men and women together has been bound to create some sparks. But there's a difference between engaging in mild friendly flirtation and being labeled flirtatious.

Mild flirtation is the kind that lets a male colleague know "I think you're funny" or "I think you're cool." Being flirtatious carries more than a hint of sexuality and almost always backfires in the workplace, usually on the woman. One study showed that women MBAs who were flirtatious got fewer promotions and earned less than their peers who did not flirt. In another study, people were shown two separate videos. In one, women displayed flirtatious behavior, like batting their eyes and flipping their hair, and wore short skirts and tops with low necklines. In the other video, women wore conservative pantsuits and had straight-forward behavior. Both groups had similar résumés. You guessed it. The flirtatious women got lower scores in leadership and job capability.

Even if you're not being flirtatious, think about what your clothes are saying at dressy business functions. If you find male executives staring at your décolletage, not your face, you're wearing the wrong dress.

Forever Young

It's going to happen to you. And it's already started to happen to me.

If you're like me, it's a subject you don't like to talk about, but you think about it more than you want to admit.

Aging.

❋   ❋   ❋

Age is not an asset for women.

❋   ❋   ❋

Anne Bancroft was only thirty-six when she portrayed the older woman, Mrs. Robinson, in *The Graduate*. And Dustin Hoffman, who was just six years younger, played someone her daughter's age!

Feeling depressed yet?

It's important to have a realistic attitude about aging because being older is a particular liability in the workplace for women. Gray-haired men can have a wise avuncular quality that's appealing to the highest levels. Few women are perceived as the office sage.

There's a lot to be said for aging gracefully. But you still need to look contemporary and like a player, so I'm all for trying to dial time back a bit by camouflaging gray hair and ditching the matronly clothes or matchy-matchy suits for contemporary styles that work with your age. But remember that nothing ages a woman more than desperately trying to look young.

Look at al the fashion attention that Iris Apfel has received. She is over ninety and has become a "geriatric starlet" and fashion icon. Known for her bold clothes and oversized eyeglasses, she is the first living woman to have an exhibit of her clothes at the Metropolitan Museum of Art in New York. At a time in her life when most people have retired, she has groupies—very young to very old women who tell her how the museum exhibit of her clothes and accessories transformed their lives and gave them the courage to develop a unique and idio-syncratic personal style. She's been transformed, too, from a private person who did her own thing with clothes to a fashion icon who others consider a style authority and who's being asked to judge fashion competitions by magazines and fashion schools.

Ten Tips for Strong Visual Identity

Okay, so you aren't a natural beauty. Neither am I. But we can still succeed. Here are ten tips for bridging the gap:

1. **Have fun and create a personal look.** Aim for a look that's distinctively you—that expresses who you are, is appropriate for what you do, and makes you feel good.

2. **Remember, likeability trumps looks.** An open, positive attitude helps you exude energy and makes you more likeable.

3. **Don't neglect your hair.** Hair is a powerful branding device so chose a style that complements your personal brand message.

4. **Have a visual trademark.** Find a signature accessory or color that jumps out and people associate with you.

5. **Project power and confidence through body language.** Adopting power poses such as standing tall with expansive arms gives you executive presence and helps you to be perceived as a leader.

6. **Cultivate your voice.** Have you ever met someone whose voice did not seem to match his or her appearance? A good voice enhances your looks, and a bad one detracts from your attractiveness.

7. **Don't follow the fashionistas.** Tip your hat to style but select something surprising, not the obvious choice.

8. **Be consistent at every touch point.** Don't send mixed messages with a polished appearance in person and a messy office or harried voice mail message.

9. **Emphasize your best features.** Look at your visual assets: hair, eyes, skin, posture, figure, hands. Which should you emphasize?

10. **Use clothes to communicate messages.** The care you put into how you present yourself is not a shallow endeavor but a powerful communication tool. It's not just for the symbolism and to satisfy the scrutiny you're under; your style conveys a powerful message of self-possession to other women, particularly junior women.

WOMEN: THE ROAD TO SUCCESS

Joi Gordon,
CEO, Dress for Success

Most people want to fit in, but ever since I was a child, I have wanted to be different and to be remembered. It wasn't difficult to do that growing up as an African American in Tulsa, Oklahoma. I was always starting things—the first black woman to do this or the first black woman to do that. For me, being part of a minority was an opportunity to stand out. It was a great experience. I went to college and law school without student loans. I finished seven years of college owing nothing.

When I came to the Bronx to be a criminal attorney, it was the first time in my life that I didn't stand out. I was one of many.

I couldn't figure out how I could stand out until I was watching TV one day. I saw a segment on Dress for Success, an organization helping women get clothes so they could get good jobs. I went in to donate some suits, and I met the founder, Nancy Lublin, who had started the organization with a $5,000 inheritance she had received from her great-grandfather. Within sixty days I was asked to join the board, and four years later I was running the worldwide organization. I had found my passion.

The premise of Dress for Success is women helping other women. I think women are wired to help other women. For women, self-confidence is very linked to the image we have of ourselves. If you don't have the appropriate clothes, you're not going to be able to do your best at the job interview. We make it easy for women all over the United States and all over the world to be a part of other women's career journey. Although we're best known for giving out suits, we want to be known for keeping women employed. That's why we have mentoring, coaching, and seminars—all the tools women need to land a job and be successful.

We're still a midsize nonprofit, so I tend to do a little bit of everything and try to do a lot with less. It could be easy to burn yourself out because there is so much to get done.

I meet with many corporate women who are interested in moving into a nonprofit job. They've made good money, but they don't feel satisfied. They don't feel fulfilled. At the executive level, nonprofits are often looking for advanced degrees: a master's or PhD. If there is a strong counseling component, it may be important to have an MSW. Many of us in the nonprofit community joined a nonprofit when it was small and had little funding and worked hard to build it into what it is today. So there can be skepticism about someone's commitment and whether they, too, would have worked as hard. I definitely think there is something to be gained for nonprofits from individuals with for-profit business backgrounds. I think all you need to see in a candidate is passion coupled with talent.

It's one thing to have a job, and quite another to love what you do. My job completely changed my life. I love coming to work. I feel that I'm helping to change the world.

Like my organization, my personal brand is about women helping other women. The women on my board, they allow me to stand on their shoulders. I've felt nothing but love from these women. For me, mentoring and networking is about helping others. How can I help you?

I feel lucky to be paid for getting and giving joy (just like my name).

Women who brand tend to develop a leadership style that's collaborative yet decisive and empowers themselves and their team.

7

THE FEMALE STYLE OF LEADERSHIP

Imagine that you and your team are working on a difficult project with a tight deadline. You brought together a varied crew to kick around solutions. You recruited junior and senior people from your group. You even invited some outside people from other departments so you could get their perspectives.

Some of the ideas are intriguing. Some are off the wall. Some are uninspired. But a junior person we'll call Bronwen came up with a terrific solution.

You're the leader who will be presenting the recommendation to top management. Do you take credit? Or do you say, "This idea actually came from a junior team member—Bronwen"?

Give Recognition, Get Loyalty

You could take full credit for yourself, as some leaders do. Who would blame you? (It's a dog-eat-dog world, isn't it?) You paid your dues slogging it out in the trenches, right? After all, you're on the hook when things tank.

That could be one way to act. Just not the best way.

While there is often little difference between the sexes in leadership studies, women seem to favor a leadership style that is more democratic, one founded on collaboration, teamwork, and recognition. More people are empowered to contribute and are recognized for it. It's a way of leading that fosters loyalty to the leader and goodwill with the rank and file.

It's easy to understand why. Praising top-notch contributors and recognizing the creators and the doers regardless of status is the "carrot principle" in action. By giving recognition, you engage all the members of your team and give them credibility with higher-ups and clients. When you demonstrate that you value others, they will value you. It's a classic win-win.

It's a more personal leadership style. This way of leading says that you value people, that you reward individual contributions and potential, that you're fair and more accessible. And this will come back to benefit you. After all, leadership is about hope. It's about the belief that, with you at the helm, things will be better and obstacles will be surmounted. If people believe that you are going to help them have a better future, they will rally around you and get the work done. And you will attract willing and enthusiastic followers and clients.

A meta-analysis of female and male leadership styles led by Professor Alice Eagly, which looked at forty-five leadership studies, found that women tend to create a different brand experience and way of engaging with others. Women are slightly more likely than men to be "transformational leaders" who seek to inspire, like a mentor or a coach. They tend to nurture and empower employees and encourage teamwork and innovation by collaborating more with people and sharing decision making. They are likely to praise and reward when projects exceed expectations.

As leaders, women have more of a big-picture orientation. They are also more intuitive in their approach to decision making and more personal in their leadership style. Of course, having a mentoring leadership style has its drawbacks, too, if you spend too much time mentoring others and success at your organization is based on other measures.

CHARACTERISTICS OF THE FEMALE LEADERSHIP STYLE

- Acting as a mentor, coach, or team leader
- Collaborating and sharing the decision making
- Being more subjective and consensus driven
- Nurturing and empowering employees
- Having a strong people orientation
- Encouraging ideas from all levels

In contrast, men tend to be "transactional leaders" who tend more toward a command-and-control style and set up an exchange-type relationship with employees. Interestingly, women did score higher than men in one area of transactional leadership: rewarding employees for good performance.

So why do more women tend to gravitate toward a more inclusive team-leader approach? Some think it may be a safer bet for women because they won't seem bossy. Branding a woman or girl as bossy has always been a devastating way to put her down. But the traits of the female leadership style also show up in childhood studies of boys and girls. When asked to solve a problem, girls are more likely to form teams and collaborate on decisions, while boys are more apt to appoint a leader who gives orders.

Now for the disclaimer. We are all different. Some of us have a more feminine style, some a more masculine style, and others an integrated style encompassing elements of both. We each need to find a personal style, one that is authentic and that works in our career. To do that, we need to understand the advantages and drawbacks of each approach as we form our own leadership style.

Write down the adjectives that define your leadership style. Think of the more typically female leadership traits: collaborative, nurturing, coach-like, inclusive, and less structured. Think of the more typically male leadership traits such as assertive, persuasive, rational, and process oriented. Which traits describe you best?

Leadership Powwow

Unlike the masculine style of top-down leadership, female-style leadership encourages bottom-up and lateral input on leadership decisions and is even more apt to cede a certain degree of control to team members. In this sense, the female style of leadership is similar to the relatively new idea of "adaptive leadership" taught at Harvard's John F. Kennedy School of Government and other places.

Rather than setting forth a strategy or vision for the company or team, the adaptive leader powwows with others to devise one together. Rather than being the chief problem solver, the adaptive leader creates a culture of problem solvers. The adaptive leader asks the tough questions and listens to other viewpoints, particularly those that challenge the traditional way of doing things.

The ability to work with others and consider alternative viewpoints is powerful. The reality is that working in silos doesn't produce the quantity or quality that results when people pull together as a team.

Likewise, a collaborative leadership style in which you share some control will get people to see you as a leader rather than a boss. A leader leads by listening and by inspiring hope and trust. A boss tells you what to do and you do it because it's part of a transaction, rather than for a loftier (read: better) relationship. In short, give orders and you're a boss. Share control and you're a leader.

A "Feeling" Leader

Our powers of empathy and our feeling approach can help us connect and engage with others as leaders. One of the key female-male differences that shows up on personality assessments like the *Myers-Briggs Type Indicator*® (MBTI®) instrument is between Thinking and Feeling preferences in making decisions.

On the one hand, people who prefer Thinking make decisions in a rational, logical, and objective way. They operate from a more detached viewpoint and like consistent rules with clear-cut causes and effects. Thinking types believe that emotion can distort decisions. If this sounds masculine to you, you're right. Around 60 percent of all men have a preference for Thinking in the Myers-Briggs assessment.

Feeling types, on the other hand, live in the gray area. They see nuance in the world. They use empathy and emotional intelligence to supplement facts and provide meaning and solutions. They have a more subjective point of view and look at situations from the inside out—taking into consideration specific circumstances and the people involved. People who prefer Feeling seek solutions that bring about harmony and consensus. They adapt to the specific situation, rather than relying on black-and-white rules. If this sounds like you, then the odds are that you are a woman. Three-fourths of women tested as Feelers in the Myers-Briggs assessment in a national study.

✦ ✦ ✦

The majority of men are Thinking types;
The majority of women are Feeling types.

✦ ✦ ✦

The Top Job

The most obvious question is, "If women have such strong leadership traits, why isn't the business world a matriarchy?"

And it's far from that. Women hold less than 5 percent of the Fortune 1000 CEO jobs. And about 15 percent of Fortune 500 corporate officers are women. That is virtually the same number as twenty years ago. Even in female-dominated industries, organizations, and groups, a male leader is often perched at the top of the organizational chart—what social scientists have dubbed the "glass escalator" for men in female-dominated organizations.

For the time being, at least in most companies and organizations of any size, the top job has "male brand" written all over it. When men and women view leaders as men or father figures, the preferred leadership personality is assertive, competitive, and directive—all culturally masculine. This leaves women in a double bind. We are not viewed as having what it takes to lead, yet if we display the same male leadership traits without tempering them with softer female behaviors, we are devalued.

What's a woman to do? As female leadership expert Alice Eagly told me, the idea that you can just rely on your feminine wiles and leadership strengths undermines your success. "Many roles, particularly leadership roles, require taking charge, being decisive, and engaging in masculine behavior. Leaders generally benefit from both culturally male and female personality qualities. Women need to learn how to be assertive, persuasive, authoritative, and, if possible, charismatic—all culturally masculine. It's the blend, the splitting the difference, that you see in so many highly successful women."

❋ ❋ ❋

You can't be a "servant leader."

❋ ❋ ❋

Besides, because women leaders at the highest levels are so rare, we women are under more scrutiny and our missteps are magnified. When women fail as leaders, it's often a failure of leadership style, not a failure of ability or experience. You have to come across as decisive and in control, with a strong people-orientation. You must resist putting yourself in a subordinate role, asking for permission, as some women leaders do. Having an inclusive style is a strength, but at the end of the day, you have to make the hard decisions and lead.

The In-Group

Ever since women began to climb the management ladder, observers have asked, "Do they have what it takes to lead large organizations?" The answer isn't as simple as yes or no.

In business, as in life, what you can't see can hurt you. Something sociologists call "in-group–out-group bias" is also in play. Bias is a challenge we all face. Most of the current business leaders—who are picking the new leaders—are men. Like members of any group, most men feel most comfortable with people like themselves, the in-group. They may have negative stereotypes about women, the out-group, but not necessarily.

The good news is that in the past couple of decades we have made some progress in changing perceptions about women in some industries that used to be male preserves. Today, we do see more female-brand leaders in professions like advertising, publishing, media, cosmetics, fashion, education, and health care, and in nonprofit organizations.

The Best of Both Worlds

Both the male and female leadership styles can be highly effective. It isn't as if one works and the other doesn't. Or that one style is good and the other is bad. Both have advantages and drawbacks.

But the best leaders have an "androgynous" style that blends the best of both male and female leadership traits. Aspects of the female leadership style are more in tune with today's global business world, where women's ability to lead and persuade diverse groups of people can be a real advantage.

Today's leaders must increasingly use inclusiveness and relationship building to accomplish goals, since team members on many complex or global projects won't report to them or their bosses. These are ad hoc teams with multiple reporting lines. Yet the person who leads the team still has to get the job done. As the lines of authority blur in today's modern companies and projects demand cooperative teamwork and things move so fast, our collaborative, relationship-building, and communication skills will be a tremendous advantage, particularly if we hone our persuasive abilities and decisiveness.

After all, the job of leaders is to create hope and optimism in their followers, what social scientists call "relational authenticity." In other words, it's not enough to communicate your values, lofty and well intentioned though they may be. You can't be a good leader unless you have followers who believe in you and your ideas, and that takes a blending of what is best in both the female and male leadership styles: being inclusive yet decisive, intuitive yet rational, nurturing yet assertive.

Define *Your* Goals

There is a powerful reason why we don't see more women at the top, and it doesn't have anything to do with ability or leadership style. Many women don't want the top job.

Attaining success at the top of a Fortune 100 company or any large organization requires extreme dedication and sacrifice. Most CEOs of large corporations work sixty to one hundred hours per week. They are workaholics by most definitions of the word, and studies show that most workaholics are indeed men.

✸ ✸ ✸

Many men at the top are workaholics.
Fewer women are willing to be workaholics.

✸ ✸ ✸

Even though some research studies show that the majority of female middle managers aspire to the top levels of their companies, successful women often tell me, as one did recently, "Yes, I'm ambitious. But not for the top job or even number two in my company. My family is important, too. It's like what Jackie Kennedy Onassis famously said, 'If you bungle raising your children, I don't think whatever else you do well matters very much.'"

So it's not just lack of role models, the female leadership style, or the glass ceiling that's holding some women back. Some women don't want the executive suite. They don't want to be superwomen who focus single-mindedly on work, as many male leaders are willing to do. It's life before work.

Careers can be more complicated for women. We have multiple roles and, arguably, richer lives. Many women have children, aging parents, active community commitments, or just an interest in staying healthy and sane. Many are not willing to make the sacrifices required to succeed at the highest levels, with frequent travel and late hours. Nor should they have to.

Ambition in More Than One Arena

It's not that women aren't ambitious. Of course we are, but we are often ambitious in a different way. Many women want a rich life as well as a great career and therefore take a broader view. As "Marci," an executive vice president of a multinational company, told me, "I want to succeed in every sense: at my job, as a wife, as a mother, with my friends, for the causes I believe in. Success for me is joy in all these things." When I asked Marci if she wanted to be president of her company, though, she told me emphatically, "No, today I'm very challenged and excited by my work, but I also need some time for my family and my interests. I would lose that if I moved any higher in the organization. So I sort of hit the glass ceiling, only it's one that I created."

And Marci is not alone. As a rule, women have more expansive interests and a more organic approach to careers, while men are oriented more toward planning and goals. Recent research shows that 60 percent of women cite a dual focus on careers *and* family, while only 20 percent of women define work as taking precedence, which is the typical male view. (The other 20 percent of women are home centered.)

Options Lead to Different Choices

When women have choices, most don't make the typical male choice, a hard-edged focus on career and money. Many choose what one female executive called the "scenic route," moving from demanding line jobs to staff positions with less burdensome workloads so that they can manage everything. And that may hurt our success and salaries, but it also allows us to concentrate on the things that are important to us. Today, savvy companies are offering opt-in/opt-out and flextime programs so that women can succeed in both spheres.

Some talented women are deciding to completely opt out, at least for a while, and others are choosing to work part-time so that they can care for children or elderly parents. When the term *opting out* first came on the scene after an article in the *New York Times* in 2003, it generated a lot of controversy because some women see it as a step backward. The topic creates a division almost along generational lines—with younger women in favor of "choice feminism," as it's been branded, and women of a certain age basically reciting the Betty Friedan playbook and warning that it won't be so easy to opt back in. But that remains to be seen. Brenda Barnes, who headed up a division at PepsiCo, traded a staff of thirty thousand for three kids. Yet she was able to stage a dramatic comeback and became chairman and CEO of Sara Lee. (There are no rules.)

Having options is always good. But let's face it, it can be difficult to opt back into the workforce after a prolonged absence unless you stay engaged with part-time or consulting work related to your career, or you go the entrepreneurial route.

Ladies' Preference

The search for meaning is a driving force for many people, particularly women. Women talk about intrinsic goals like making a difference, having an impact in their communities, or doing good in the world. We want jobs that jibe with our values. And this often separates us from men. A 2005 study involving five hundred dual-income families showed that the quest for meaning and job autonomy becomes more prominent as a woman's level of education increases.

Contrary to what you might think, the closer our work comes to the male model in terms of extreme time demands and responsibility, the less satisfied we are. Indeed, there has been an exodus of women from extreme jobs in law, investment banking, and technology in which workaholic schedules are the norm. These women are looking for challenge, meaning, and a kinder, gentler world.

While it's correct to challenge stereotyping of individuals, it's foolish to deny gender preferences. One famous study involved 34,000 people on a kibbutz in Israel in the 1970s. The idea was to create a utopian community with no sex-role stereotyping. Every job on the kibbutz was equally divided between men and women.

But it didn't stay that way. Gradually the men and women chose the jobs they preferred: 70–80 percent of the women chose people-oriented jobs working with children or in education, while men chose more systems-oriented jobs in factories, farming, construction, and maintenance. So much for utopia.

The preference and talent that so many women have for people-related work do not sit well with some women, since they think that pushes us into lower-paying jobs. But the higher you go in the business world, the more important people skills are in determining your success. You can't be CEO or president of a company of any size unless you get people to follow you by rallying your team and building relationships with key clients and managers.

The Creativity of the Woman Entrepreneur

Many women exit corporations to become entrepreneurs or self-employed service providers to satisfy their desire for meaning, passion, and self-determination (not to mention cold, hard cash).

American entrepreneur Sara Blakely was a part-time fax machine saleswoman and a part-time stand-up comic who wanted to look svelte with no bulges or telltale panty lines showing when she wore slim pants. So she chopped off a pair of pantyhose and called her shapewear creation, "Footless pantyhose. But then a few years later she came up with a saucier name, Spanx, partly for its "virgin-whore tension" and partly for the "K" sound. In the early days, some retailers were so offended by her product's name that they hung up the phone when she called to pitch her shapewear line.

But she persisted and revolutionized the shapewear category. She introduced lightweight girdles called Power Panties, legwear called Tight-End Tights, and casual separates called Bod a Bing! to name a few of her creatively-named product lines. Today, Blakely is the wealthiest self-made female billionaire.

Measuring Brand Effectiveness

As a woman who is aiming for success—however you define it—one of your goals should be to engage people. Just as marketers strive for brand engagement connecting people with their product at every touch point, you should engage people with your product—Brand You.

✺ ✺ ✺

Getting honest feedback is a key to mastery.
Men are more likely to speak candidly to other men,
so women often don't get the candid coaching that can be so valuable.

✺ ✺ ✺

Be smart and establish a mechanism for getting feedback. Marketers do this all the time with the screens that pop up after a transaction online inquiring about the customer service you received. Since it can be difficult for women to get tough feedback from male managers, encourage critiques without being defensive. Another way is to set up a feedback loop by calling a few attendees after a meeting you led and asking, "How do you think the meeting went?" Then listen without being defensive.

People who engage others quickly are what social scientists call "clickers." When you have a good conversation with someone, you feel that you have clicked with them. A kind of mutual syncing takes place, so there is a kind of mind meld. One way to speed up clicking is by being open and revealing who you are as a person. One of the best ways to click with others is through the power of imitation. Quick social bonding comes from mimicry. It's usually unconscious, but you'll need to start out consciously at first, until it becomes second nature. Use similar words, gestures, and movements as the person you are talking to and you'll find it creates a vibe of goodwill.

Little gestures can be big brand builders, too, like handwriting a short, thoughtful thank-you note to an employee for a job well done. One executive I know keeps the notes she's received in a special pouch for a pick-me-up on those days that things aren't going so well.

Adapt Your Brand

As a self-brander these days, you have to be prepared for just about anything and be ready to get your brand back on track quickly if it derails. The gap between job levels is larger the higher you go. The very talents that made you a great company treasurer—such as a fanatical attention to detail—are not the qualities you need as company president. Leaders who micromanage can't lead.

Every level demands a different type of leadership and brand experience, and different smarts and focus. People at the top of an organization need a more outward and big-picture brand orientation. You're representing the company brand to the outside world, after all.

At the highest level, you need to focus on strategy and execution but not get mired in the details. You need to inspire and motivate yourself and your team to win.

You'll also need to recruit a strong team, not loyal yes-people who will make you feel safe. Doris Kearns Goodwin's book *Team of Rivals* is a great management primer on leadership and team building. Rather than paying back his chief rivals in the presidential campaign by banishing them to political Siberia as most politicians do, Abraham Lincoln gave his rivals cabinet posts! He formed a team of his former rivals—the best and the brightest politicians—who were willing to criticize him and help him lead during that troubled time in American history. Lincoln nurtured and empowered his cabinet members so that he could take advantage of their collective intelligence and experience, characteristics of the female-oriented leadership style. President Obama mimicked Lincoln's srategy when he appointed former foes to top jobs in his cabinet in 2009. And it can be a very smart leadership strategy. Leaders deaf to criticism and surrounded by yes-men can be a recipe for disaster.

There is a strong consensus that diverse groups lead to better problem solving and decision making. One interesting study found that men surrounded by other men of similar status jockey for the alpha role and are more likely to make high-risk financial bets. Women are not affected by this type of peer pressure. Another study tested the saliva of male financial traders to track testosterone levels during the day. The study found that higher testosterone levels could lead men to take higher risks, even affecting their ability to make rational decisions. So be the type of leader who encourages diversity of thought.

You could also consider working with a leadership coach. (Corporate icons and celebrity endorsers have a slew of coaches who help keep them at the top of their game on the public stage.) The best choice would be a mentor with no agenda other than your success. You'll also run across people who are on a similar journey—spiritual and emotional soul mates—people who can teach you things or give you the courage to step up and take a stretch assignment.

Check for Brand Fit

Opportunities generally look scary at first. That's why most people pass them by. Sometimes, somehow, in our gut, maybe, we feel opportunity when everyone says to beware. When you feel it's right, take the leap.

Research shows that women are less likely to succumb to the "vividness bias," selecting a job because of bragging rights, such as a prestigious firm's name or a stupendous salary. Instead, they are more likely to take a holistic approach, looking at issues such as collegiality, travel, and office location.

It's wise to make sure the company brand and culture fit with your brand and your lifestyle needs. Some "opportunities" can be a wrong turn and hurt your brand if you don't figure out how to mesh with the two. Look at Katie Couric. She left her leadership post as the reigning star of morning talk shows to take on the role of first woman anchor of the network evening news. Evening news was traditionally the place for gravitas, so it seemed like a smart move, and Couric was brought in to lure women and young people to the evening news on CBS.

This career move tarnished Couric's image since the serious CBS evening news format didn't capitalize on what made her a runaway success—her engaging style (backed by her high-wattage smile) of interviewing and talking to people in a casual format. Couric moved back to daytime television to host her own talk show. Then she jumped to Yahoo as its global anchor to capitalize on the rise of the Internet for instant news and punditry.

There's no playbook that works for everyone. It's a dynamic world, and the career marketplace is never static. That's why it's important to stay tuned in to what's shaping your marketplace, and keep your eyes open. Maybe your career will be a straight trajectory upward, but maybe not. Maybe you'll want to take some detours along the way, or even opt out for a period.

The career strategies that worked in your twenties and thirties may work when in you're in your forties or fifties, but maybe they won't. Or maybe the geographic area or industry you've targeted for Brand

You is not as relevant today and you have to find the new high-growth ecosystems looking for talent.

Or maybe you're interested in other things and want to relaunch your brand in a new direction. If you're thinking like a leadership brand, particularly a female leadership brand, you can deal with whatever comes your way.

MADE IN AMERICA

Muriel "Mickie" Siebert
founder, Muriel Siebert & Co., Inc.

Only in America could my story take place. When I came to New York, I had five hundred dollars and a very used Studebaker car. Today I have eighteen honorary doctorate degrees even though I never completed college, and I became the first woman to buy a seat on the New York Stock Exchange.

I have an affinity for numbers and analysis. I can look at a page of numbers and they light up and tell me a story. When I started out on Wall Street, there were no women there other than the secretaries. I started out as a trainee in research at an investment firm and had to change jobs twice because men were making considerably more, or almost twice as much as me. Not long afterward, a major financial institution called in a commission order. They said they made money on a report I wrote. I was not registered at that time but later obtained my license. Since the major financial institutions valued my research, that meant that I could make money, and it gave me faith in myself. Being able to make money was important to me because my father died without money. We had to move from a nice house to a one-bedroom apartment, and we needed my uncle's financial help to support us.

On the job, I had to be flexible and learn to speak two different languages. To fit in on the trading desk, where every third word was a four-letter word, I had to talk like the guys, but for my clients, institutional portfolio managers, I was the complete opposite: analytical, thoughtful, and proper.

As a woman then, there were no female role models, so I just blazed my own path. It may have taken longer to build my clients' trust, but being a woman also helped me because it was so unusual at that time— I was unique. Part of my career goal was "Where can I go where there is no unequal pay situation?" That's why I decided to buy a seat on the stock exchange and work for myself.

Besides making money, I wanted my career to be about "How can I use my talents and abilities, and make a difference?" In 1975, on the first day members of the New York Stock Exchange could discount commissions, Muriel Siebert & Co., Inc., opened as a discount broker-age firm and later became the only woman-owned NYSE brokerage firm with a national presence. In 1977, I was appointed the first woman superintendent of banks in New York State, a position I held for five years. While I served as superintendent of banks, my firm was in a blind trust.

Now I am developing and sponsoring financial literacy programs for youths and adults, not just on investing but on the basics, which include credit cards, checking accounts, and income tax returns. These subjects are usually not included in required courses in schools. I want people to understand the basics of personal financial literacy. Their paychecks will go further, and we may be able to prevent another sub-prime mess from developing.

Women who brand build a network
that's broad like men's networks tend to be
and selectively deep like women's networks tend
to be.

8

BORN TO NETWORK

At its core, networking is about connecting with other people, and that's something women excel at. Connecting is in our DNA. Given that we have the social gene, it's surprising that many career women don't have a great network, while many men do. Women often have a tight group of women friends but lack the big network of casual business acquaintances that men specialize in, and that's something we need to think about changing if we want to create more success in our lives.

We women tend to favor deep relationships with a group of close friends, a preference evolutionary scientists trace to our roots taking care of the family and the home. We also see this preference in playground studies: Most girls tend to pair up and play one-on-one with a single playmate, while boys are more likely to play with a series of different mates and then go off and play with a larger group. When girls are in their teens and hormones kick in, the preference for intimate relationships with a small group of friends accelerates. The urge to connect deeply is something that stays with us our entire lives. These close personal relationships are extremely fulfilling to women because the connection is strong, deep, and committed.

❉ ❉ ❉

Women connect intensely *with* small *groups.*
Men connect superficially *with* large *groups.*

❉ ❉ ❉

A small group of deep relationships provides a reliable source of support and advice. But in the wider world of careers and brand building, a small, though intensely committed, group is not as advantageous as a large network of contacts, even if they are superficial.

The Male Networking Model

The male social model is very different.

Whether it comes from years of helping one another score in team sports or it's in the male DNA, guys understand the mutual advantage of helping one another out. Men may talk about the Giants and the Jets or the Red Sox and the Yankees, but then business and the arranging of favors often follow. Many men can know someone casually or hardly at all and think it's no big deal to call him to arrange an informational interview or pitch him for a specific job opportunity. They feel comfortable pitching a friend or the friend of a friend.

While women favored close relationships, from an evolutionary point of view, men's specialty was forming a large network of shallower relationships. These broad networks were vital for developing social systems and culture. So while most studies view women as more social, men are social, too, just in a different way.

Men, on the whole, seem to lack the need for deep connection. Not that they don't connect deeply with a significant other or buddy. It's just that men more commonly connect in a way that's more superficial from a woman's point of view. In fact, many of us would hardly consider many male connections to be "relationships" at all. But male networks are powerful because of their size and range and men's comfort with making and accepting professional contacts. It gives them a major advantage in marketing their brand in the world.

✸   ✸   ✸

Men run in packs.
Career women should, too.

✸   ✸   ✸

There's no reason we women can't expand our relationship model to connect with more people on a less personal and less intense level. And many successful women have. But we all need to do it if we want to compete at a higher level or open up more career options.

Obviously, if we can form deep relationships, building a network of shallower acquaintances should be like playing in the minor leagues. And it's a smart strategy because the reality is that you can't do much on your own or with only a few supporters. We need to employ our connecting strength in a different way so that we can achieve real networking, and we have to understand its value.

Join the Networking Economy

After all, networking involves an economy. It's a hidden economy, but a very powerful one. It's an "economy of favors."

Networking is a bit like a business transaction, a system of informal quid pro quo. The networking trade works like this: I do you a favor, and the unspoken understanding is that if there is an opportunity to repay it, you will. A networking economy works only if there's trade back and forth. Otherwise, everything will come to a halt. It's an economy that men know well and many women are just learning about.

Strong Network = Career Capital

We all like to believe that career success is based on merit, but that is only a starting point. The truth is that participating in the networking economy will make you richer in terms of options and opportunities and, most likely, financially, too. Your network is like the brand alliances marketers form. If you don't understand how it works and don't participate, you will lose out on the opportunities and knowledge that others—your competitors—have.

For some women, networking transactions seem like a big deal. We may be more reluctant to ask for something unless we know someone well. But the best networks feed on lots of superficial relationships, and most people are willing to help. It's often as simple as phrasing it in terms of a "favor." A Stanford professor found that when he asked people to fill out a questionnaire in Penn Station, 57 percent agreed, but when he prefaced the request with, "Can you do me a favor?" 84 percent agreed.

Women have been saddled with the reputation of being self-centered and not very helpful to others, particularly to other women. But I think that is largely a thing of the past and has been greatly exaggerated. Of course, many of us have run across women with this affliction—the queen bee syndrome. These are women who made it and don't want other women to come close to their position on the totem pole. As Madeleine

Albright said, "I think there is a special place in hell for women who don't help other women." (And it's not one of the nicer places either!)

The exchange of favors is what psychologists call "reciprocal altruism." A reputation for helping others and doing favors is an asset that attracts others to you.

Favor givers are attracted to those who reciprocate and punish those who take a favor and don't reciprocate. Believe me, the word will get out on what kind of person you are.

So if you have a reputation for helping others with contacts and professional information, you will be more successful because people will want to help you, too. Some women at the top of the networking game tell me that they often have to explain the networking economy to the women they are helping. Otherwise, it doesn't occur to them to reciprocate.

Ask and Want Not

When I talk about the networking economy, women often ask me, "How do I ask?" "How do I approach people?" "What are the words I should say?" In my experience, men don't labor over this as much. Men are more comfortable tapping a superficial acquaintance for a favor without all the soul searching and self-doubt that women go through. Maybe one reason is that in traditional dating, men have more experience socially in asking and women don't. But we don't have to undergo shock therapy to get good at it.

Sometimes, all you have to do is ask for help. You can say, "I'm wondering if you can help me," and then you make a specific request. But most of the time you will need more finesse, especially if you want to seek help for bigger things. After all, unless you know someone very well, you can't call up and ask, "Can you help me get a job at your company?" or "Would you be my mentor?" or "Will you give me your business?" That's tantamount to asking, "Will you lend me one hundred dollars?"

A more natural approach is to ask, "Can I brainstorm with you for fifteen minutes over the phone about how to move from my job to the next level? I know that you transitioned into various jobs in your own career, and I'd love to hear more about it."

The secret is to ask a question, allow the other person to talk, and then follow up with another question. Most people love to talk about their careers and offer advice, as long as they feel you don't expect them to get you a job. But as the relationship develops, you might ask if you can approach them from time to time as a sounding board. Then presto, you've got a mentor. And chances are high that your mentor will introduce you to others who will be valuable in your career journey. Just make sure to figure out ways to reciprocate!

Episodic Networking Syndrome

A lot of women think of networking as an important job-search technique. And it is. So when their jobs look dicey, they start networking madly to find a new one. Once they do, they go on their merry way until the next job dislocation, when they start networking madly again. It's sort of like yo-yo dieting—lose weight, gain weight. About the second or third time you do this, your network starts feeling used, and you're up the creek. (I suspect we all know a lot of people with this syndrome.) In short, network before you need to.

Successful networkers take a long-term rather than a short-term view. Networking is about meeting and connecting with people, sure, but it also is about access and leverage. It can be access to people: people on the inside of a company you want to join, people in power or with the capital to invest in your venture, people who know lots of people, people who are looking for the talent you offer, or people who have the talent you need for your team. It can also be access to information. The higher you go in your career, the more you will be expected to be at the forefront of new ideas, deals, alliances, and opportunities for your company. Networking can put you in touch with the latest ideas and trends in your industry. It can help you tap resources that will keep your company in the lead. This sort of information gives you enormous clout and leverage.

So don't think you're done when you have a great mentor. In reality, you need a broad network of contacts and alliances. And you don't build it by thinking of what they can do for you. You build a powerful network by thinking of what you can do for the people in it.

Networking PhD

One of the savviest women networkers I've ever known (and I've known a few) was Phyllis Cerf Wagner. When Phyllis joined the ad agency, I was working on the "I Love New York" advertising campaign. Things were in a bit of turmoil since Governor Hugh Carey, who had championed the campaign, was leaving office.

Phyllis was a highly visible fund-raiser (a form of networker) for former mayor Ed Koch, who was running for governor. But Koch didn't win. Mario Cuomo did. It was an upset victory, and I was worried that we might lose the account. A change in management always puts an ad agency in the danger zone.

Phyllis used a lot of female strategies in her business networking. She played "matchmaker," connecting people she thought could benefit from knowing each other. She nurtured client relationships, sending handwritten notes and making frequent phone calls to check in on people. She gave little gifts, often insignificant in price but thoughtful, like a recipe, an article, or a book she thought the other person would be interested in. Phyllis's pièce de résistance was hostessing parties in her home, inviting business associates, politicians, authors, and media and entertainment people. They were something to behold!

Initially, Phyllis didn't have a network with the new governor or his team. Gradually but steadily, she developed relationships with all the different levels of the incoming New York State team. She even made introductions to celebrities and government leaders such as Frank Sinatra and Henry Kissinger, who appeared in our new commercials. So we held on to the account, and Phyllis taught me that you don't have to be born into a network. You can do it the old-fashioned way—earn it.

Five Networking Tips

Here are five tips I've developed from observing great networkers like Phyllis:

- **Make a human connection.** Find an area of common interest so a real relationship takes hold.
- **Seek out people who are different than you.** It's more advantageous for your professional growth to meet people of different backgrounds and from different places.
- **Give little gifts.** When you meet someone new, lock in the relationship by following up with an article, an introduction, whatever might be useful.

- **Act like a hostess.** Walk up to people you don't know at a business gathering and introduce yourself with a warm smile and a strong handshake. It takes confidence, but people will appreciate you for it.
- **Find out the best way to stay in touch.** Some people like to be contacted by phone while others may prefer e-mail or texting. Ask them.

Network Far and Wide

Today there are women's networking groups of all types. There are industry groups for women. Many companies are supporting internal women's groups and funding speakers, workshops, and events that promote more female leadership. While men network on the golf course, women are putting together nontraditional women's networking groups through book clubs, knitting clubs, manicure groups, you name it.

✳   ✳   ✳

All-female network = weak network.

✳   ✳   ✳

Since there are more men in positions of power, you'll need to have a lot of men in your network, too. Explore industry and business networking groups, political clubs, and nonprofit groups so that you'll be able to meet interesting and established women and men.

Networking can happen anywhere. One colleague left her job after a long career as president of a major company. Not sure what she wanted to do next, she made an unusual bet with herself. She vowed to say yes to everything that came her way over the next six months. Someone asked her to go with a group of volunteers to cheer up women prisoners over the holidays. Now she really didn't want to go, but she kept her promise, said yes, and went anyway. On the bus to the prison, she began chatting with another volunteer. And that conversation and connection led to a whole new career teaching at a university.

There's also something about old school ties. School affiliation can be so valuable as a networking tool that it's worth considering the quality of the university's alumni networking program when you choose a school. How good is the alumni database? What kind of networking and job support are available to graduates? It's the same with many sororities. A professional friend, Jill, told me that every job throughout her career came from a contact through Chi Omega sorority, but not necessarily women in her chapter. Once a sorority sister, always a sorority sister.

No Network—No Security

Power networkers realize that you need the help of all kinds of people on the road to success. You'll find that the more varied your network is and the more people you know, even casually, the more opportunities will come your way and the more help will be there when you need it.

Here are the four key networks that can play a significant role in your professional success. In my experience as a coach, many women, even senior women, concentrate on deep relationships with *Grass Roots*, a small tribe of close business and personal friends (the lower right quadrant). This can be a problem if you are ambitious or in a job transition since you are swimming in a very small pond.

Women Who Brand cultivate a strong *Career Champions* network, a strategic network consisting of senior executives (mentors and sponsors) and people of around your level who are allies or connectors. These two networks are *your narrow/deep networks*.

The two networks on the left side of the chart, your *Core Contacts* of business associates inside and outside your company and *Weak Links* network, acquaintances that you don't know very well, are your *wide/shallow networks*. These should be your largest networks since these are casual relationships, and social media and the Internet can be good ways to stay in touch with the occasional note or article.

Here are some thoughts on how to use the special kinds of relationships in these professional networks.

Career Champions: This is your informal "board of directors," people who advise and talk you up. It's a mutually beneficial relationship so look for ways to help them too. In addition to mentors and sponsors, networking stars also seek out *allies*, a band of professional colleagues who help one another succeed. You can even formalize your tribe of allies by having monthly or quarterly dinners or meet-ups. The final component is *connectors*, plugged-in people who know a lot of people. Your Career Champions group is your most important network and should be constantly expanding as your grow in your career.

Grass Roots: These are your close business and personal friends and family who are your confidants—people that you have on your speed dial. They are people you trust and who know you well. What they may lack in prestige, they make up for in the support they provide.

FOUR Key Networks

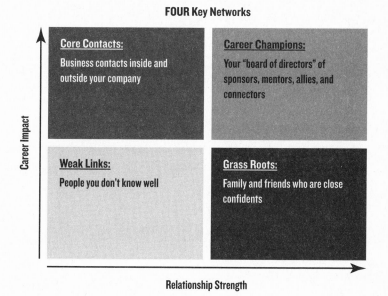

Core Contacts: These are business associates inside and outside of the company. Volunteer for committees, join employee resource groups, and seek out task force assignments to expand your contacts at work or in your industry.

Weak Links: The people in this network are weak links because you don't know each other well, but don't ignore them. A weak link is often the source of a fresh job lead or introduction because you don't travel in the same circles. When I look back on my career, most of my job opportunities came through weak links, people whom I had met through friends or at networking events.

The Social Network

The career network you've worked hard to build in person can be made more valuable through virtual networking. Business managers search online for their employees. Recruiters research prospects online. Colleagues Google one another. Others want to reconnect with people they lost touch with. People don't have to know you well to "like," "friend," "subscribe," "follow," or "endorse" you online.

Social media like LinkedIn and Facebook magnify networking like never before. Social media is like in-person networking on steroids. LinkedIn is the world's largest professional network, with more than 100 million members and counting, so it has to play a leading role in your online networking tool kit.

LinkedIn is built on a series of powerful networking ideas: the power of connection, the value of an introduction, and the multiplier effect of virtual networking.

To make the concept of a personal introduction a socially powerful idea, the organizing principle of LinkedIn is *degrees of separation*. So you have first-degree (direct) contacts, second-degree contacts, and so forth. What's astounding is how quickly your contacts can snowball when you tap into the contacts of your first-degree contacts.

To harness the networking power of LinkedIn, you'll need to master making requests to link, asking for help, and making introductions. Otherwise, you've just got a list of names with contact information like you'd find in a phone book.

❋   ❋   ❋

*Use LinkedIn to link up with current and prior
acquaintances, to request and make introductions,
and to request and make recommendations.*

❋   ❋   ❋

When you want to meet someone in your extended network on LinkedIn, you request an introduction. Just as with traditional networking, you need to ask directly for something specific and to focus the request not on why you want to be introduced, but on how you can add value to the contact you want to be introduced to. So it's not, "I want to meet your friend Kara because I want to sell her something,"

BORN TO NETWORK 127

but "I am interested in meeting Kara because we have a new service that her company's competitors are using that I think she would want to know about."

You can use LinkedIn to send someone a "little gift," an article or link that you think they would find interesting. LinkedIn gives you a platform to display recommendations and endorsements. Reach out to business colleagues and associates and offer to write a recommendation on LinkedIn for them. Most will want to reciprocate and write you a recommendation. Even easier, use LinkedIn's endorsement feature, which allows you to click and endorse people for specific skills and abilities.

It's smart to participate in LinkedIn groups or start your own group. Choose groups that are relevant to your industry, job function, and interests. Groups are a valuable way to keep up with the buzz in your industry and areas of interest as well as meet new people. You can post questions, sign up for weekly digests, and start discussions.

Segment Your Social Networks

While LinkedIn will play a central role in your virtual branding and networking, there are other social platforms that you should use too, each with its own strengths and abilities. Here's one way to look at the key social sites:

- **LinkedIn:** Use it for positioning and promoting your career identity and building your business network.
- **Twitter:** Use it as a PR tool to build your visibility and build positive perceptions of Brand You through short message bursts.
- **Facebook:** Use it to keep in touch with close friends and family—people you already know and want to share your personal life with.
- **Pinterest:** Use it for "pinning" wonderful images that amplify who you are, your interests and values.
- **Google+:** Use it to meet new people who share your passions and interests and to segment your followers into "Circles."

It's a big world out there and you can be a big part of it with your virtual and in-person networks in tow.

NETWORK, NETWORK, NETWORK

Pamela Paton
senior vice president, State Street Corporation

"Don't think you have to stay at one company" is the advice I give to women just starting their careers, even though I stayed at the same firm for over twenty-five years. I think it's vital for young people to explore options, find out about companies, find out who you are. This exploring usually involves shopping around for good fits and opportunities. I was able to do that, luckily, at the same firm, State Street Corporation.

I grew up about one hour south of Boston in blue-collar Taunton, Massachusetts. Dad died when I was seven, and by the time I was sixteen, I was working. My Depression-era mom was always stressing the importance of working hard and becoming successful. I put myself through college and started working for a program run by a major medical center, but they lost their contract and I was in need of an opportunity—fast. Networking paid off, and I was offered a job at State Street in Boston.

Moving from Taunton to Boston was a big move for me, but success is all about big moves. And I was ready for it.

Your boss can be very important in your career, and my first boss at State Street was great. She was a mentor as well as a boss and encouraged me in my entry-level job to be patient. "Something good is coming, perfect for you." It did come, in the form of traveling the country selling a revolutionary new product. I often felt amazed that I was this junior person representing the company alone with this important new product. They had confidence in me because they could see I had confidence in myself. I loved selling, not for the thrill of having a conquest, as may motivate men, but because of more female traits like caring for clients and helping them be successful. I viewed it as win-win.

I wasn't always in a good situation, though. After one company move early on, my new boss seemed to have an agenda of making a lot of changes, and I thought those changes might not be good for me. I was careful to network within the company so that others knew I was talented. I was able to zigzag out of that department and get back on track.

My advice to young people is to find a mentor. Find multiple mentors who will give you strong, constructive criticism, key people both inside and outside the company, both in the area where you work and out of it. Try to find people that you look up to. I've had a few that were my boss. Some others I approached. I would tell them why I admired them or how I enjoyed working with them on a project. And I'd ask, "Could you give me an hour a month?"

I would also suggest that you must be willing to take risks. My turning points came from taking risks by moving around in the company. I looked for opportunities to learn new business areas and skills, and if something looked good, I threw my hat in the ring. I was also willing to make lateral moves that may not have seemed like advancing, but if I saw potential in another department, I was willing to leave my comfort zone and do something new. And I never regretted it. Sometimes the best way to get ahead is by making a sideways move.

Having a wide network inside and outside the company gives you power. Seeking out mentors gives you wisdom. Zigzagging can make you more valuable.

Change can be stressful, but not changing could put the brakes on your career, and that can be stressful, too.

Women who brand don't give up.
They retool their brand and relaunch.

9

A BRAND FOR ALL SEASONS

Attractive and slim, wearing a chic pink Chanel suit, "Ophelia" cut an elegant image when we met. It was quite a contrast from the phone conversation we'd had a week earlier, when Ophelia emotionally described being laid off.

Up until that day, Ophelia was headed straight up the career ladder. From a family of Chinese American professionals, she attended prestigious schools and started her career in finance after business school. Life was sweet for several years, until the subprime mortgage crisis hit; then Ophelia was out on the street.

The economy was in the doldrums with no end in sight, and the financial services industry was undergoing a major retrenchment, with thousands of talented people being laid off. Ophelia diligently sent out her résumé and got no bites—not even one. And to make matters worse, no one even bothered to return her phone calls.

Do What the Branders Do

Ophelia had a classic marketing problem. As good as her product (Ophelia) was, her current positioning was no longer in demand. She couldn't go to market until she relaunched her brand around a good idea that fit the current market.

But when I asked Ophelia what her dream job would be, I could not believe her reply. Her goal had almost no relationship to what she had been doing or what she was looking for now. Ophelia's dream was to work in the luxury goods industry. Her twist was that she wanted to help Western luxury goods manufacturers market to the new money elite in China.

It was an interesting idea, particularly from a brand strategy perspective. The U.S. economy was bad, and the financial services sector was undergoing a wholesale restructuring. Tens of thousands of jobs related to real estate and financial services were vaporizing. But in China, the economy was stronger.

Just like a marketer who looks overseas for growth when the domestic market is bad or mature, Ophelia had a compelling rationale for repositioning her brand for a growth market.

Ophelia's first challenge was to develop a personal-brand strategy and marketing plan that would point her in the right direction. Our first problem was Ophelia's glaring lack of credentials. We had to do a brand makeover. After all, Ophelia had no business experience in Asia whatsoever, nor had she lived there, but she did have an interest because of her Chinese heritage. And she had no experience with luxury goods other than as an avid shopper at Chanel and Prada.

Your Brand Is What You Make It

We came up with a novel solution that would give Ophelia something akin to experience and get her brand back in demand. The idea was to conduct a market research study to measure perceptions of U.S. and European luxury brands that Ophelia could represent in China. The study would cover all the companies on Ophelia's hot list of places to work—from Ralph Lauren to Prada to Burberry to Louis Vuitton.

✻   ✻   ✻

Brand makeover: Connect
the dots to a new Brand You.

✻   ✻   ✻

Then we drafted letters to these luxury goods manufacturers, telling them that Ophelia was off to conduct a study of the high-end and "affordable" luxury market in China and was including their brands in her study. Ophelia offered to meet with them and share her findings after she completed the study. She even got some "financing" from a friend who was a successful entrepreneur, which covered the cost of the trip and the research in return for access to her findings.

Ophelia got responses from twelve out of the first fifteen companies that received her letter—a truly astounding response rate. Rather than looking for a job, Ophelia was offering something of interest to her target companies. Her success was no doubt propelled by the feeding frenzy of Western firms tapping the newly affluent segment of the Chinese market. It was clearly the right thing at the right time.

Before Ophelia went to China, she called or e-mailed all the people she knew who had business contacts there and asked them to arrange meetings. Every time she met with someone, she tried to get two or three additional names of people to meet. She also pitched people she didn't know, telling them what she was doing and asking for a short meeting. Before she knew it, Ophelia had practically every breakfast, lunch, and dinner spoken for and an impressive roster of business contacts in China, including many in the budding luxury goods market.

The Chinese businesspeople Ophelia contacted were hungry to build contacts with the West, so they were receptive to her calls—a very different situation from what she'd faced just a few months earlier, when no one had returned her calls. Plus Ophelia was packaged perfectly for the part, with her sassy haircut and classy clothes, and her ability to bridge East and West based on her background, language ability, and heritage.

Ophelia's strategy worked. Doing the market research gave her credibility with her new brand positioning, and by the end of her month-long stay in Shanghai, she was an expert on the luxury goods market in China. She knew which brands had the greatest cachet, and which didn't. She knew who the likely buyers were, and how to woo them.

This may sound like maneuvering, probably because it is maneuvering. We're all trying to maneuver in our careers, but most of us do it in a haphazard way or rely on wishful thinking. It's smart to maneuver strategically so that you can meet the people you want to meet, even if your goal isn't as bold as Ophelia's.

Fluid Branding

Whether you're developing your overall brand strategy or specific marketing tactics, think of it as both an analytical and a creative process. You have to use the rational left side of your brain to look at yourself objectively as a "product" in a broad marketplace. But brand strategy also employs the creative right side of your brain. And when you tap into your right brain, you open the floodgates of creativity that will help you position your brand and take more chances.

✹ ✹ ✹

Thought + spark = new Brand You

✹ ✹ ✹

Marketers develop business plans for their brands, and you should do the same for Brand You, but realize that plans are an organic thing. You can't plan everything. You'll change, industries will change, or the market will change, as Ophelia found out. You can't possibly predict all of it, and you'll have to make adjustments along the way. But you can't accomplish anything without some planning, so be sure to do periodic assessments and revise your action plan.

As one female executive told me, "Some women are process oriented, so they want a checklist for success, but career success is not a defined process. There isn't a one-size-fits-all formula. I can't tell them, 'Spend this percentage of your time on this, and that percentage on that.' What I tell people who work with me is, 'Figure out the results you want, and then figure out the best way to get them. You've got to create your *own* brand and visibility track. What worked for me won't necessarily work for you.' Part of my self-brand strategy is to find a 'mess,' something that isn't working, and offer to take on the assignment and fix it. Then I move on to a new mess."

Zig When Others Zag

As a branding rule of thumb, when everyone is zigging, it's usually smart to zag, particularly if you are the lesser-known brand. In the 2008 Democratic presidential primary, Barack Obama faced a formidable, more experienced, and better-connected foe, Hillary Clinton. As a member of the Democratic establishment with a husband who had been president, Hillary not only had a strong, differentiating brand position built on experience but was well known (high brand awareness) and, to boot, had most of the deep-pocketed Democratic fund-raisers sewed up (strong brand alliances).

The political race was the equivalent of Coke versus Pepsi.

So what did Obama do? Like a small brand battling against a better-known, more experienced, and better-financed competitor, he zagged. He found the white space his opponent wasn't occupying. His brand idea was "Change" against Hillary's "Experience" positioning.

Rather than going after traditional Democratic fund-raisers and donors, Obama zagged and found the white space there, too. He built his fund-raising mostly around middle-class donors—many were people who had never contributed before to a political campaign—and did his prospecting primarily through the Internet. More than 90 percent of the campaign's cash came from donations of $100 or less. Obama introduced tactics like Obama University, where first-time fund-raisers were trained in raising money and community organizing. Soon, he had a grassroots and Internet fund-raising machine.

Visibility Pays

You'll also want to gain visibility in some arena if you want to build a brand that's in demand. When something is visible and well known, we tend to think it is better than something that is not as well known. We attribute more positive traits to familiar things, and we're more likely to buy them even if we've only heard the names of the brands and know nothing more!

Women are notorious for being visibility challenged. Many women undervalue the importance of taking credit for accomplishments, volunteering to lead projects, or getting to know a range of senior executives.

Don't be afraid to toss your hat in the ring. Ask for assignments, and volunteer to lead or be a part of projects and new initiatives. When "Bria" was a beginning employee, she was itching for a promotion. "I didn't have all that much to do at the time, and with little to do, I get bored and restless, so I asked around for more work. One Friday, a helpful executive dropped a pile of reports on my desk and said, 'Why don't you write a summary of these?'"

Bria had a lost weekend, and the executive had a full report on Monday. He did it again, and she did it again. And before long, Bria was promoted to a bigger job. A little extra work can pay off a lot. So don't be afraid to ask.

When you're an important contributor or leader of a project or initiative, don't relinquish ownership, either—you can always share ownership. Remember the lesson of John Adams. Adams ceded the task of drafting the Declaration of Independence to Thomas Jefferson because he thought Jefferson was the better writer and regretted it for the rest of his life. "Jefferson ran away with the all the stage effect," he lamented, "and all the glory."

Visibility means you're more likely to show up on Google when someone plugs in your name. Look at "Julia," who held a series of senior management positions in retailing. When a PR release about a new company initiative went out, Julia would tell the PR department to get a quote from one of her key lieutenants, not from her. Her recognition of subordinates made her a popular boss, but you can take it too far.

Now that Julia is in transition, she is virtually nonexistent on a Google search, and that's a problem. There's no paper or virtual trail to accentuate her impressive job history, so her role is diminished in the eyes of headhunters and prospective employers. Julia's competitors are other senior people with similar job histories who do have an impressive list of news clippings and links at Google, and that makes them more desirable.

Wendy Who?

Then there's Wendy, who worked at a large, global company for more than five years but hadn't been promoted to vice-president, as had some of her colleagues who had similar responsibilities. Part of the feedback Wendy received from her boss was that she wasn't "ready" and needed to have a higher profile in the company. Like many women, Wendy was so laser focused on the job and leading her team that she was virtually unknown outside of her department. She was the invisible woman.

So how do you change that? After all, you can't run an ad with your picture on it on the company website.

Here are four fixes that Wendy did to stage a comeback and get on the radar screen at her company. First, Wendy pitched herself to be one of her company's brand ambassadors, the high-profile band of company veterans who represent the company at job fairs and industry conferences. They also promote the company virtually as bloggers and by posting short tweets about the company as members of its Twitter tribe.

Wendy's second action was to volunteer for a global cross-functional team set up around a key initiative. This put her in contact with colleagues outside of her comfort zone (and geographic zone). Wendy also got involved on the program committee of an important industry association. It was an avenue to get acquainted with colleagues at other companies and also to suggest (and meet) speakers for upcoming industry events.

The other thing Wendy did was improve her online brand on LinkedIn by including links to her posts on the company blog and her tweets. Eventually, she pitched her boss for a promotion, something she had never done before. (Remember, be a woman who brands.) Wendy was no longer waiting for him to tap her on the shoulder like some knight in shining armor and bestow the VP crown on her head.

The Visibility Ladder

Visibility building can be viewed as a ladder—each level gives you more leverage. The first step may be as simple as getting out of your office. As "Jennifer," a senior exec at a technology company told me, "One of my missions is to encourage women to build visibility in our company. I tell them, 'Get out of your cubicle. Pick up your laptop and spend some time working in the lounge so you can meet people in other areas.'"

We often meet new people and form the ties that bind at these impromptu meetings. You find out what's going on at your company. You learn about shifts in power. You learn about new initiatives in which you can play a role. When you're seen, you're a contender.

If you are an employee, you can use nonprofit activities for building higher-octane visibility. Offer to chair a fund-raising drive, join a nonprofit board, or chair a committee. Many of these activities are covered in the local press, plus you will meet other interesting and successful people.

Nothing gives you more prestige and visibility than being on the board of a recognized corporation or nonprofit, since most boards are still an elite boys' club. Just as women are poorly represented at the highest levels of American business, women hold about 15 percent of Fortune 500 board seats. A board seat gives you visibility and top-notch contacts as it broadens your experience. It will give your career a big boost, so seek it out when you're moving up the ranks. As one female board member told me, "Men seek out board seats at the height of their careers. Most women seek out board seats after they've retired. So they don't get the bang it could give their career."

Visibility is especially important when you're in transition or if you decide to opt out while raising your children. Many moms have impressive academic and career credentials, and being a mother gives you a certain amount of management cred, too. As Madeleine Kunin, the first and only woman governor of Vermont, said, "If you've organized a birthday party for a five-year-old, you can run a political campaign." But it's even smarter to keep some visibility in the business world by taking on consulting projects or even forming mommy SWAT (Smart Women with Available Time) teams. These all-mom teams are put together through temp agencies or, even better, by the moms themselves, to tackle business projects, usually on short notice with drop-dead deadlines.

The Best Self-Promotion Doesn't Seem Self-Serving

I don't buy into the adage that "all publicity is good publicity." As a self-brander, you want your brand-building and visibility tactics to lead to positive impressions about you. As in the world of branding, nothing is as powerful as word of mouth, and it's free. And good buzz generates more good buzz because we are all influenced by what others think.

Recently, more than 14,000 people were asked to rate new songs. One group was shown just the titles and the musical groups and asked to rate the songs. Then a second group was asked to rate the songs but was allowed to see how many times each song had been downloaded by the first group.

Surprise! The opinions of the first group had a profound influence on how the second group rated the songs. The second group gave higher ratings to the songs the first group had liked, creating a snowball effect around the top picks. Positive word of mouth influences us all. It's as if a lightbulb goes on in our heads—"Gee, if other people say such wonderful things about her, she must be good."

It may be difficult to get on *Meet the Press,* but most of us can learn how to work the virtual room. And it's a valuable talent to cultivate, since Internet resources like blogs, websites, social networks, and e-zines are incredibly efficient for building visibility. And with today's hectic lifestyle, in which time is limited, leveraging the power of the Internet to build visibility and connections is smart.

If you work for a company, though, make sure you're in compliance with the company philosophy. Some companies encourage citizen bloggers as long as they don't post anything proprietary or damaging to the company. If you're an entrepreneur, however, visibility should be part of your lifeblood, and the Internet should be a core part of your visibility strategy because it's a low-cost way to promote yourself.

Public relations, whether digital or the old-fashioned media kind, is largely an ecosystem that works on relationships. Pitching a great story or sharing fresh insights on your blog is important, of course, but relationships make it much more likely that others will notice your pitch and put it on their media outlets or be receptive to mutual links.

Success comes to those who build a community around a distinct niche. In order to enter the media space effectively and build an audience, you need to check for room in the channel. Find a different spin, different content, a different attitude, a different something. For your PR efforts to be successful, whether through traditional media or new media, the "news" and the views it creates must not seem self-serving, nor must you appear to be keen on self-promotion. It pays to have a camera-ready sound bite when you're interviewed, but you must not come across like a person who's panting for publicity. As the saying goes, "If you drool, you lose."

Tend Your Reputation

Contrary to what we might think, people remember the bad over the good. Perceiving a bad event lights up the brain rapidly in MRI scans. That's why we can remember vividly where we were when very bad events like the 9/11 terrorist attacks occurred but not much about what we were up to when a happy event occurred.

That's why good reputations take a long time to build but a short time to destroy. You have to *build* a reputation by racking up a lot of achievements and positive perceptions over time, but a high-profile fall from grace can blow all that good work to smithereens.

And to make things worse, bad reputations not only spread quickly and erase years of good deeds but are hard to shake. Bad reputations are sticky. That's why brand managers guard a brand's reputation and move quickly to remedy a problem before it gains currency.

★   ★   ★

Negative reputations are hard to peel off.

★   ★   ★

Not that you can't rebuild a brand after a fall. You can, but it isn't so easy, and sometimes the damage is permanent unless you can present a good redemption story. Look at public figures who got caught up in scandals. Martha Stewart spent some time in prison but was able to relaunch her brand, and today she's back at the top of her game, as strong as ever. Perhaps her "crime" didn't seem so bad in the scheme of things. Plus there is the sense that she came through the experience stronger and more human. Remember, Americans love redemption stories.

Get Engaged

Brands wouldn't exist without advertising and the media. *Brand engagement* is one of the hottest ideas in media today. Engagement is the process of building a relationship between individuals and a brand by making the brand message and the way it's delivered so personally relevant that people can't help but react to it. And smart marketers try to build strong brand connections at every touch point.

Advertisers use the term *engagement* especially for Internet ads and Internet videos, in which a visual or verbal stimulus grabs viewers' attention so that participation allows them to interact with a brand on a deeper level. Just think about it. The combination of responding to and interacting with an ad or message is more powerful than just viewing an ad.

Indeed, advertisers are even trying to measure engagement using brain-scanning technology similar to what neuroscientists use to study social and emotional reactions. When we are engaged by an ad, clusters of brain cells fire off in the same regions of the brain that react when we experience something pleasurable, like talking with someone we love. So it's no wonder advertisers are starting to use the million-dollar MRI machine to study the iconography of their brand in the minds of consumers. This helps them create the best visual stimuli, messages, and emotions and put them in the right context.

From a branding perspective, engagement is extremely powerful. It's one thing to be aware of a brand, say, by hearing its name or seeing it in TV commercials. That's why brand awareness is the first leg of the brand journey, and marketers measure awareness. But it's something else again to be engaged by a brand, to click through and view a video, for example, and forward it to your friends.

Imagine the difference between two leadership styles, one leader is very aloof and formal, the other is very open, friendly, and interested in people. She is interested in knowing about projects you're working on and even remembers your husband's name and the ages of your kids when she runs into you in the elevator. Who has the better brand engagement? Brand engagement is all about interaction and personalization. It works for brands and it will work for you too.

Strong Brand = Pricing Power

The strongest brands have pricing power. You want to have pricing power, too, or people will think you are Brand X.

When something is more expensive, we think it's better than something that's cheaper. This may or may not be true in reality. Look at this wine taste test in which volunteers were asked to evaluate five wines. Each bottle was labeled by price: $5, $10, $35, $45, and $90 a bottle. Naturally, everyone liked the most expensive wines best. Even the brains of the taste testers noticed the difference! Brain scans done as the tasters sipped and rated the wines showed that the expensive wines generated more activity in the area of the brain that responds to pleasurable experiences.

In reality, the wine labels were deceptive. The same expensive wine was in the $90 and the $10 bottle, and the $5 wine also was in the bottle labeled $45. But although these wines were the same, the brains of the testers registered less pleasure when they thought they were drinking a cheaper wine!

High price gives people an image boost, too. You will be assumed to be better than someone who is paid less.

Being paid well and feeling worth it professionally are relatively new for women. And the salary gap is changing for younger women, particularly in large cities. The old gender gap was the pay gap. In

2007, women's pay, on average, was 80 percent of men's pay. But the gap is narrowing for women in their twenties. Census data from 2000 through 2005 show that women in their twenties made 89 percent of what men were paid. Amazingly, in big cities like New York, Dallas, Los Angeles, and Chicago, twentysomething women are making more—up to 20 percent more—than men.

Don't Give Up

What's the difference between those who go on to become brands and do great things, and those who don't? Mom called it the two Ds, drive and determination, traits she felt were key to success. Psychologists call it "self-efficacy"—a powerful belief in yourself, no matter what. Self-efficacy is different from self-esteem, which is an overall feeling of self-worth.

Self-efficacy is the unshakable belief that you've got what it takes and will succeed if only you persist. It's keeping the faith until you figure out how to retool your brand and get traction with your target audience. It's telling yourself positive messages and not magnifying negative ones. (The brain builds new synaptic connections if the process is repeated enough.) It's not letting setbacks defeat you.

Remember, smart brands don't give up. They retool the brand and relaunch.

Brands typically go through a cycle that looks like a bell curve. The breakout period of high growth and visibility is followed by a mature phase and then a gradual decline. As you can imagine, it's one thing to get plum opportunities and visibility when you're young, new, and different, and quite another to get them when you're mature and no longer fresh and exciting. But masters of brand durability find ways to stay relevant and visible long after most brands fade from view. You can, too.

Remember, all brands—both people and commercial products—go through periods of struggle, sometimes very long periods of struggle. Take solace in the company you have during the tough times (and the great stories you'll be able to tell about your struggles and comeback). In Julie Andrews's autobiography, *Home*, she recounts a screen test she did for MGM when she was twelve years old. "They needed to gussy me up a bit because I was so exceedingly plain," she revealed. With a hairstyle of ringlets mimicking Shirley Temple's, she took the screen test, only to be told, "She's not photogenic enough for film." If J. K. Rowling had given up after her twelfth rejection, people would be saying, "Harry who?" Rowling ditched her first name, Joanne, and rebranded herself as J. K. because the publisher felt that a book aimed at boys but written by a woman wouldn't sell as well.

So if you feel like you're in a maze with no good place to go, keep forging on until you find the right opening. After all, it's the journey rather than the arrival that brings the greatest satisfaction. It's like the experiment with the monkey and the grape. The monkey feels the greatest reward not when he eats the grape but when he is sure that it's in his possession. And if things aren't working out, you can always rebrand yourself for a second act.

A Woman's Brand

The notions of self-creation and remaking one's brand are very American notions, practically a founding principle of this country. And there are second and third acts in American life. As one journey is ending, it is time to repositon yourself for the next phase, as Hillary Clinton did so well in her presidential bid concession speech in 2008.

Hillary Clinton's speech began, like the good ones do, with a bit of self-deprecation. "Well, this isn't exactly the party I'd planned, but I sure like the company." She went on to thank all the people who supported her, wrapping her thank-you in our most popular myth, the American dream: "the moms and dads who came to our events, who lifted their little girls and little boys on their shoulders and whispered in their ears, 'See, you can be anything you want to be.'"

Hillary told stories in sentences so well crafted that you felt you knew these people. She asked her followers "to take our energy, our passion, our strength and do all we can to help elect Barack Obama the next president of the United States." And she took a page from Obama's own playbook to say: "Yes, we can!" She capped off her description of the work that remains with a rallying refrain repeated in commanding cadences: "That's why we need to help elect Barack Obama our president." She seemed so ready to help Obama that she might even be willing to answer the phone at 3 A.M. for him.

Hillary reached out to women, young and old, many of whom had tears in their eyes, and reminded them of what had been accomplished. "Could a woman really serve as commander in chief? Well, I think we answered that one." And later in the speech, in a memorable visual metaphor, "Although we weren't able to shatter that highest, hardest glass ceiling this time, thanks to you, it's got about 18 million cracks in it. And the light is shining through like never before, filling us all with the hope and the sure knowledge that the path will be a little easier next time." Hillary saluted the suffragists at Seneca Falls in 1848 and all the women who fought for women's and civil rights, leading to the refrain, "because of them . . . , because of them. . . ."

The speech was as much about Hillary and her women legions as it was about Obama, but she did give an acceptable amount of praise considering how new it was for her to be an Obama supporter. It was a speech big in scope, graceful in wording, inspiring in vision—the speech of a statesperson, not a politician. Later, Clinton was given the chance to show her statesmanship, when she was appointed secretary of state in 2009.

A Brand for All Ages

There are no hard-and-fast rules for successful branding or successful leadership for women. You'll have to use your own brain and instincts, your female-based aptitudes, and your special uniqueness and abilities—that's what makes it fun and interesting. But here are some guidelines to keep in mind as you take your female brand out into the world:

- Sunny beats gloomy.
- Sparkle beats drabness.
- Authenticity beats pretending.
- Consistency beats muddled.
- Difference beats conformity.
- Strategy beats luck.
- Tactics beat inaction.
- Engagement beats aloofness.
- Visibility beats a low profile.
- Perception beats reality.

Just as no two people are the same, even if they are twins, no two people have the same brand assets. As a self-brander, your job is to manage the asset that is you through the good times and the bad.

The good news is you are in charge of your brand—in crafting your brand and taking it out into the world. You are the brand manager and the creative director. You are the screenwriter and the editor. You get to select the core brand concept, your message, and the direction (including changes in direction) for your brand. (The bad news is also all of the above.)

Tap into your powerful woman's intuition and instincts to help you zero in on new ways to keep your brand in demand.

Create the brand that is right for you and the action plan that takes you in the direction you want in your career as well as in your life, that complements your motivations and aspirations, that takes advantage of your female mindset and your personal inclinations. When your brand is focused, relevant, and engaging, people will take an interest in your success. You will be maximizing your most important asset—you.

DREAMS ARE FOR LIVING

Meenu Chhabra
president and CEO, biotechnology company

My childhood was full of mixed messages about the role of women in society. My mother, like my father, had a PhD, but she lived the life of a traditional Indian woman. Mother always told me, "You are equal to any man," but she knew that she was not a role model for gender equality.

My background made me determined to lead by example as well as words in my life. I strive for bold and clear communication in my career and urge women to speak in a large voice and never be intimidated by male bravado.

My mother's acquiescence to the status quo when she had so much potential caused me to strive aggressively for high achievement. I was twenty-two by the time I finally rebelled against my father's backward ideas and had my first date. I trained as a neuropsychopharmacologist and earned an MBA.

My goals in life were fueled by desires to travel and to create things that hadn't existed before. I first worked in Italy but then moved to a Swiss multinational pharmaceutical company, which allowed me to travel the world and learn about deal making and cultural differences.

I was often the youngest person as well as the only female in meetings. This helped strengthen my brand as being exceptional. Being young and female can help open doors, but then you need to prove your ability to stay there. I knew I was destined to run a company like I'm doing now. Working in the biotech field on vital, breakthrough endeavors like curing disease is a dream come true. It's always challenging to be a CEO, but being young and a woman compounds those challenges. My strategy is to find brilliant people and let them know that I depend on them to teach me things. I'm not an isolated figurehead, and I can be wrong. I want them to feel that they can say anything to me.

Women's lives are often more complex than men's. Women have more to juggle besides their careers. They generally have the primary role to play with the children and the myriad things that take place in a family's life. So women have to think in terms of what's important to them and then simplify their lives around that. When I mentor ambitious women, here's what I say:

- **Determine your priorities.** If your first priority is your children, focus on situations that will give you maximum quality time with your family.

- **Create a career goal.** If your goal is to become a CEO, determine when you would like to achieve that and build a plan backward from there.

- **Get a career coach.** Objective advice from someone without an agenda is crucial.

- **Identify personal champions.** It is vital to create personal champions who are senior, well connected, and respected—people who can alert you to leads before anyone else knows about them.

• **Treat your job search like a business deal.** Know the terms you would like and identify partners willing to give you those terms.

"You are equal to any man" is no longer an abstract notion for women. There are gender issues, of course, but more and more those differences are recognized as strengths.

I've learned there are no limits. I have a lot more I want to accomplish as CEO, but I also want to sail around the world, grow olives in Spain, create great photographs, raise a beautiful child, and be an inspiring example.

Women who brand know that
it's not up to other people to uncover their great deeds.
It's their job to make their accomplishments known.

10

IT'S UP TO YOU

Gender difference mirrors fundamental concepts of reality: negative–positive, matter–void, yin–yang, male–female. We're all a product of many things—our time, our place, our family—but it would hard to dispute that nothing is as fundamental to our identity as our gender.

After centuries of gender "Dark Ages" with a profound anti-female bias regarding personal independence and individual success, women have finally achieved an enlightenment of sorts. Nowadays we're seeing women's firsts fairly frequently: the first women to head a major automobile company, the first women to head the Federal Reserve Bank, and so on, until having a women in the key leadership role is no longer news.

We Still Have Some Catching Up to Do

For years women arrived at Harvard Business School with high test scores, just as the men did, but almost immediately their grades began to fall behind. Turns out, the women did well on tests but they lagged badly in class participation, which is often 50 percent of the final grade. As one HBS female professor said, the lagging performance of its women was a "dirty little secret" that perplexed administrators.

In most school situations, it's the girls who are eager to participate and raise their hands in class and generally outperform the boys. But not at the top. In the rarefied atmosphere of the Harvard Business School, alpha males, often from leading investment banks and hedge funds, dominated class discussions and the women tended to recoil.

In 2010, Drew Gilpin Faust, Harvard's first female president, started a program designed to address the gender performance gap.

The business school put monitors in the classrooms to ensure accurate record keeping of class participation. It also provided private coaching for the women, including group classes on topics as mundane as hand-raising.

Coaching Can Make a Difference

The women's equity experiment did make a difference. The female grade gap substantially disappeared. The class of 2013 was the first to graduate under the new system, but it remains to be seen how these women's careers stack up once they are out in the real world. As one female professor said, "Are we trying to change the world 900 students at a time, or are we preparing students for the world in which they are about to go?"

The HBS test reminded me of a meeting I had a couple of years ago at a well-known global investment bank. A senior HR professional there told me that she was concerned about the "incompetence" of the new women hires. All were graduates of top business schools but they weren't doing as well as the new male hires. They had the ambition to succeed but they weren't as assertive or confident in meetings or in building business relationships. It sounded like the Harvard Business School conundrum.

Of course, there are a lot of exceptions, but men are more comfortable competing, being assertive, and projecting confidence than women. Assertiveness and confidence are traits that we associate with leadership, so it's important to master them if you want to be a leader. As we saw in the HBS case study, in settings where women are actively encouraged to compete, say in all-girls schools, we see more competitive, confident women.

Self-Concept and the Big Fish–Little Pond Theory

The HBS women and the female investment bankers were victims of what social scientists call "The Big Fish–Little Pond Theory," a concept popularized by Malcolm Gladwell in his book *David and Goliath*. The psychologist Herbert Marsh created the metaphor of fish in a pond to explain the idea conceptually. Fish are only aware of their relative size compared to the other fish in their pond, and the biggest fish thinks it is really big.

We form our self-concept not globally, by comparing ourselves with all the other people in the world in a similar situation to ourselves, but by comparing ourselves to people nearby who are in our situation (our pond). So in the elite, perhaps cutthroat "pond" of Harvard Business School or a global investment bank, it is easy for women to compare themselves negatively even though they are very smart and talented. The problem is they are surrounded by people who are very smart and talented (and maybe more aggressive, too) so they feel like small fish in a very challenging, very competitive big pond.

Here's why the pond you choose is so important. Each group always achieves an average performance, and those who are above average benefit with a positive sense of self, while those who are below average experience a negative effect on their self-concept. So what matters is not how smart you are, but how smart you *feel* in relation to others at your school or company.

We prefer to associate with others whose abilities are similar or slightly better because it has a positive influence on how we see ourselves. Unless you can swim with the sharks or are in an organizational culture that actively supports diversity, it's better to be a Big Fish in a Little Pond. Social scientists find that the boost in self esteem and performance due to the Big Fish–Little Pond Theory applies across cultures and various types of organizations.

Visual Identity + Verbal Identity + Actions = Brand

We can convey who we are through our words, through our actions, and by the way we present ourselves to the world. Language can be powerful—the words we choose, the pitch and power of our voice—but that's not the whole story. Nonverbal communication is often even more powerful than what we say. Our demeanor—what we project through our body and facial expressions—says more about us than our words.

Professors at Harvard Business School have also been studying the power dynamics of nonverbal communication. When animals attack, they go "big" with a wide stance. Likewise, when people go "big," taking a wide stance with hands on hips, they convey power and dominance. As discussed in chapter 6, power poses like standing tall with a wide stance, leaning in, or take a wide stance while seated increases testosterone and decreases the stress hormone cortisol. And the change in body chemistry makes you feel more powerful, and that's communicated to others.

One interesting thing about the power pose studies is that they work even if you only do the poses for a couple of minutes *before* a meeting. Again, there's a change in testosterone levels that makes you feel more powerful, confident, and prepared.

Power poses can be an important tool to use in meetings, on the telephone, or when preparing for presentations to help you feel more confident and project gravitas. After all, even if you have a great message, it won't come across as a great message if you can't deliver it well. A powerful delivery is as important as the words are.

Fake It Until You Make It

There's another tool that, like power poses, can help you project power and confidence, even if you don't feel either of these emotions. It's called "fake it until you make it." *Shark Tank* television star Barbara Corcoran seems to have understood the technique of "faking it" early in her career.

After cycling through more than twenty different jobs in her twenties, Corcoran landed in New York City determined to succeed in the real estate business. Corcoran's company was tiny, with just eleven apartment sales in 1981; she was a newbie to real estate, and hardly an expert at the time. But she noticed something interesting. The high-end residential market was a very secretive world. It was dominated by ladies in mink coats who had keys to the best apartments, and the hush-hush nature of the business meant there was no reliable information on the sales prices of apartments.

Corcoran saw an opportunity to "fake it" and to brand. She added up the sales and divided by eleven and came up with $254,232. She rounded it and came up with $254,000, which she labeled as the "average New York City apartment price." She branded the one-pager she put together, "The Corcoran Report," made sixty copies, and sent it to every reporter at the *New York Times*. The next Sunday, on the front page of its well-read real estate section, was a feature article that began, "According to Barbara Corcoran, president of The Corcoran Group real estate company, the average price . . ." Previously a nobody, Corcoran and her company became the experts on New York real estate overnight. Faking it helped her make the big time.

During the real estate slump of the mid 1990s, Corcoran found another clever angle to invigorate her business when she read in the *New York Post* that Madonna was pregnant and looking for an apartment. Although she had no celebrity clients, Corcoran bluffed again and quickly banged out a news release with a short list of the buildings Madonna *ought* to be looking at, and sent it to all the late night news shows in New York. She used a hypothetical to brand herself as the celebrity broker and the media bought it. She appeared on CBS in New York introduced as, "Barbara Corcoran, broker to the stars!" Corcoran never did get Madonna as a client, but she got a call from Richard Gere's agent, who asked if she had time to meet with the actor, and then her celebrity client list was launched for real. Corcoran later sold her company for over $70 million.

What is the lesson here? Faking it until you make it can pay off. After all, your opinion may be just as valuable (or more so) than those of the so-called experts.

The Impostor Syndrome

"Faking it until you make it" is a good tool to use if you feel that you're not good enough. All of us have been there. If you haven't, it might be time for some soul searching.

When I was a graduate student at Harvard University, I felt a bit like a pretender. Intimidated by the Harvard brand, I thought that I was surrounded by people who were brilliant, sophisticated, and confident (in other words, Little Fish–Big Pond). I was sure that I didn't measure up and I worried my professors and colleagues would figure out that I was a fraud. I'm sure you can appreciate the kind of anxiety that negative self-image brought about.

I had the "impostor syndrome," a mindset that is associated with smart, high-performing women who have trouble internalizing their accomplishments. Despite a track record of achievements and competence, successful women can be convinced they are "frauds" and will be found out. Common feelings are "I don't belong here" or "I'm not as smart as people think," and they attribute past success to luck or think of it as a "fluke." I shared my feelings with my friend Margaret, who introduced me to the concept of "fake it until you make it." Her advice? "If you don't feel adequate, then just pretend that you're smart, confident, and in command. And pretty soon you will be." You know what, over time the negative demons left. I didn't have to fake it anymore. I learned a basic truth about perception. Thanks, Margaret.

But it's not as if self-doubt is banished forever. When I launched my company, SelfBrand, I started speaking on personal branding and women's leadership to groups both large and small. In the beginning, particularly with large audiences, I'd get the "I'm not good enough" frights. Then I'd think of Margaret and the lessons I learned, and stride confidently on stage.

Take a Seat at the Table

You don't have to feel like an imposter to feel that you don't fit in. Many women who work in male-dominated industries like technology, finance, and manufacturing talk to me about feeling like an outsider in their companies. As Claire, a computer programmer, told me, "At every meeting, I'm the lone female with a dozen guys. Before the meeting starts, the men seem to be having a marvelous time bantering about sports, so I start out watching on the periphery. Then the meeting starts and even through I'm seated at the table, I'm really on the sidelines watching."

The isolation of feeling like you are the only one who doesn't belong can be a self-fulfilling process. You want to be a player, but standing by while others are actively engaged only increases your feelings of having been intentionally left out. Claire wondered why her male colleagues didn't reach out to include her, but she didn't do any reaching out herself either. Women are more adept socially, but we often don't apply these skills at work to build business relationships or take part in the pre-meeting chitchat that can be so important in getting to know people.

Claire needed to "take a seat at the table," not just sit there but visualize herself as an actively engaged, even passionate, participant. Even with all our verbal ability, many women don't feel comfortable with "guts ball," putting your ideas out passionately and pushing your points. Taking a seat at the table with the guys also means being willing to listen to direct feedback—even if it isn't polite. But it's all a part of leadership. Taking a seat at the table can be challenging, messy, or bold, but that is the nature of leadership and women have to get comfortable with it.

What Is Your Brand Experience at Every Touch Point?

Brand experience is an important concept in branding. Marketers get involved in experience design so that there is a common and branded interaction with the brand at every touch point. That way consumers have a consistent, special brand experience.

Compare the experience of being in an Apple Store with the experience of buying a laptop or high-tech gear at Computer World. Or consider the experience of shopping at Chanel versus shopping at the Gap. Or think of having a coffee at Starbucks compared with having one at Dunkin' Donuts. Each company is building a brand image and a brand experience that's distinctive—from product design to retail experience, from the type of salespeople to the bag you walk away with after a purchase. They are creating a brand experience that subliminally, or not so subliminally, echoes the brand's big idea, or unique selling proposition.

You create a brand experience every day by the way you interact with people, the impression you create when you lead a meeting, the way you decorate your office, the way you answer the phone and talk to clients and colleagues, and the meeting notes you send out. In short, you do it at every touch point in your career life.

Think of all the touch points with colleagues, with employees, with more senior people, with clients. How can you enhance the experience to build your brand? For example, if you are trying to build a connection with someone new, do you walk her to the door after a visit in your office, or do you let that person wander back alone? Are you consistent in the brand experience you convey, or do you convey different impressions depending on whom you are with?

Don't neglect the touch points of your virtual brand. The center of your social media universe is LinkedIn, the premier business site that will be viewed by more people than you realize. Make sure that you put up a complete profile with all the keywords and skills that people might use in trying to locate someone like you. LinkedIn continually expands the site adding new features to make it more effective as a business marketing and networking platform. But if you're ambitious, you can set up a personal blog or website, and use Twitter and other social media platforms.

Another source of inspiration on how to be a female leader has always been to study the masters, to look at effective leaders and see how they have managed their personal brands. (And observe ineffective leaders for pointers on what not to do.) Whether you're observing people firsthand at work or following high-profile people in the news, you'll find that branding lessons are everywhere if you have a branding mindset.

Jump at the Opportunity to Brand

Marissa Mayer was employee number twenty at Google and its first female engineer, a distinction that Mayer made the most of in her self-branding. Besides her gender, Mayer stood out in one other very important way at Google: she was an "articulate geek," two words that rarely go together. So Mayer was tapped as the spokesperson and public face of the company. This made Mayer not just the highest-ranking woman, she was the most visible person at Google. She was soon perceived as a Silicon Valley superstar and the leading force behind the design of the Google home page and its search product.

If you were to do a SWOT Analysis of Marissa Mayer, you might put intelligence, work ethic, ambition, communications ability, visibility, and attractiveness in the strengths column.

Of course, nobody's perfect. As her fame grew, colleagues started griping about her management style and details were leaked anonymously to the media. So in the weakness column of our SWOT analysis, we could put taking too much credit personally for team projects and a tendency to micromanage every detail, causing delays not to mention a long line outside her office. Some critics cited a lack of warmth.

Over time, the negatives became a threat to her success at Google and Mayer's career stalled. She was moved from overseeing the search engine to overseeing location and local services, which in Googleland is like being moved to Siberia. Ever adept at image control, Mayer put a positive spin on the situation and positioned her new role as "managing more people."

Having cycled through four CEOs in rapid succession, Yahoo was again in search of a CEO and Mayer was on the short list. Mayer did her homework and won over the board with her well-researched, detailed presentation for the CEO slot; she had a plan for every piece of Yahoo's business. The same day Yahoo announced her as their new CEO, Mayer pulled out a trump card for the female brand and revealed that she was pregnant. In her first year in office, Yahoo's stock price doubled. She is credited with rejuvenating the Yahoo culture through a series of smart deals that brought in new blood. She has instituted other changes like offering free lunches and other perks common to high-flying Silicon Valley companies.

As a strategy to deflect criticism of her management style—her perceived coldness and her reputation for micromanaging—Mayer promulgates a brand persona as "geeky and shy and I like to code." After all, if she's a geek, that explains away most of her negatives: many male CEO geeks are known for micromanaging and often lack proper social skills as well.

The Power of Nonverbals in Branding

Michelle Obama is too savvy a woman not to use the powers of visual identity to her advantage. We haven't talked about a First Lady's clothes this much since Jackie Kennedy was in the White House. From Obama's arm-baring dresses to her love of bright colors, she has a distinct fashion sense and uses the power of her style to communicate confidence and personal power.

Obama fluctuates between high fashion and mall fashion, wearing designer clothes one day and off-the-rack duds from J. Crew or H & M the next. When she goes couture, she tends to wear the clothes of newer, often lesser known, immigrant American designers. Jason Wu, Isabel Toledo, Narcisco Rodriguez, and Thakoon all were made famous by her patronage. In a way, she's sending messages with her clothes not unlike the messages of her husband.

The First Lady's body language can communicate volumes, too. They say a picture is worth a thousand words, and the "selfie" seen 'round the world, taken at the memorial service for Nelson Mandela, was priceless. In the picture, a stern-faced Michelle Obama was captured next to the president and the Danish prime minister smiling and laughing as they snap a self-portrait on a smartphone. Michelle Obama didn't give in to the nonsense of the moment and her body language screamed, "I don't like what's going on." The president of the United States acting like a giddy teenager was seen by many as inappropriate. Michelle Obama had the right comportment for Mandela's memorial event. Her brand went up; his went down (at least temporarily). Whatever you think of her politics, Michelle Obama's brand stands for powerful, independent woman with strong convictions.

What French Women Know

Christine Lagarde is the first woman to head up the International Monetary Fund and the first women finance minister in France. She's often found on top ten lists of the most powerful women in the world and also on top ten lists of the best dressed women in the world. Five feet eleven inches tall and with striking silver hair, Lagarde has a visual identity that projects style, gravitas, and power.

Of course, Lagarde's brand isn't based on looking the part (though it helps her tremendously); she has strong communication style as well. Interviewers have gushed over her eloquent, even seductive, communication style, which features large intakes of breath to make important points. Others have commented on her propensity to cite Voltaire or Rousseau to make a point.

Interestingly, she became the first woman to hold these high-level finance positions, yet she didn't have a degree in finance or economics, but in law. Lagarde is no doubt a master networker. Being appointed the French finance minister gave her finance bona fides that she leveraged in order to be considered to be head of the IMF. But Lagarde didn't leave things to chance. She led a proactive marketing and networking campaign for her IMF candidacy, crisscrossing the globe to drum up support with leaders in developing economies like India, China, and Brazil as well as with Western leaders. (Vive la France.)

The Appeal of Mutti

While Angela Merkel is not stylish like France's Christine Lagarde or America's Michelle Obama, she has a powerful visual identity just the same. She is known for her practical yet colorful jackets that reinforce her level-headed political style. If you line them up, the jackets appear to be almost a uniform; they all have a similar cut and style but are in different colors. She found a look that works and that makes her wardrobe selection easy and efficient.

Merkel also has an unusual visual trademark. It's a hand gesture, the triangle-shaped way she folds her hands, called the "Merkel diamond" or the "Triangle of Power." When asked how she came up with the gesture, Merkel explained that there was always the problem of what to do with her hands, and the gesture had a certain symmetry. The finger rhombus is so associated with her that many of her election posters didn't have a picture of Merkel's face but just the hand gesture next to slogans like "Stay cool and choose the chancellor" and "Germany's future—in good hands."

So how did a pastor's daughter who grew up in communist East Germany end up as Germany's first female chancellor? Regarded as Europe's most powerful leader, Merkel has cultivated a brand that is no-nonsense, rational, and pragmatic, all qualities of the scientist she was trained to be.

But Merkel isn't all business. She injects softness, a nurturing quality, and humor in her communications and this has helped endear her to the German population. With austerity programs being implemented in some EU countries, Merkel seems to allude to imposing austerity at home on her website. Describing baking for her husband she says: "My cakes always have too little streusel for his liking," referring to the mixture of sugar, butter, and flour that is sprinkled on German cakes.

Merkel's image has a certain nurturing quality reminiscent of a practical, hardworking aunt or mother. So it's not surprising that early in her career her political enemies poked fun at her somewhat matronly image, calling her "Mutti" ("Mommy"). But now it's a term of affection that Germans use for Merkel, though she has no children of her own. Another popular phrase, reflecting the belief that she will make the right decisions, is "Mommy will sort it out." Merkel's brand emphasizes her pragmatic philosophy and "step by step" approach to problem solving. Whether her leadership impacts Europe's staggering current problems remains to be seen, but her leadership brand is already proven.

A Head-to-Toe Metamorphosis

It may be superficial. It may be unfair. After all, why should we be judged on our looks?

In reality, people make snap judgments about us based on looks every day. That's why it's important to package yourself to advantage. Plus, there's an added benefit: researchers believe looking good makes you feel more self-confident, and that pays off in more success.

Not many women admit to having a facelift, and neither does Dilma Rousseff, Brazil's first female president. But it can be hard to deny, given the scrutiny that high-profile women like Rousseff are under. Media reports claim her extreme makeover included a facelift, eyelift, and dental treatment, along with visits to a trendy hair stylist, cosmetologist, and makeup stylist.

Her serious, tough demeanor was thrown out the window when she underwent a makeover as she prepared to run for president of Brazil. She had dental work done to fix her teeth and give her a softer smile. This was reportedly followed by plastic surgery to her face and eyes to make her look younger. A hair stylist lightened her hair color and gave her a stylish cut in the mode of Venezuelan fashion designer Carolina Herrara. Makeup experts redid her eyebrows and makeup. She replaced her eyeglasses with contact lenses.

It was a dramatic transformation for Rousseff, who grew up in an elite family but became a Marxist guerilla in her teens fighting the country's military dictatorship. She was thrown in jail for two years. After her release, Rousseff rebuilt her life and entered politics. When she was elected president, she was asked whether she wanted to be called "presidente," a term that can be used for both men and women in Portuguese, or "presidenta," used for women only. She chose presidenta with the feminine ending. In her inaugural speech she promised "to open doors, so that in the future many other women can also be president."

Personal Branding Ideas Can Come from Anywhere

Sometimes you can stumble across a clever personal branding idea accidently. Madeleine Albright, the first female U.S. secretary of state, was holding discussions with Saddam Hussein and the next day in the Baghdad newspapers, she was denounced as a serpent. Since she had a snake pin in her wardrobe, Albright thought it would be fun to wear it on her jacket to the next negotiating session.

Everyone had a good laugh over the serpent pin but the reaction triggered an idea to Albright about how her pins could be a communication and diplomacy tool. When the sessions were going well, Albright would wear her butterfly pins or an American eagle. When little progress was being made, she'd wear a row of turtles. Often reporters would ask her, "Madam Secretary, how are the negotiations going?" And Albright would say, "Read my pins."

Albright became so closely identified with her pins that other heads of state would give her pins when she visited on diplomatic missions, and she would search out unusual pins as she traveled around the world. Later Albright realized that the pins weren't just a fun communication tool, they were a great personal branding device. In her book and the traveling exhibition, *Read My Pins*, Albright recounted how people would sometimes mistake her for the reporter Helen Thomas or even Margaret Thatcher. But with her pins, she had a visual hook that made her personal brand identity immediately recognized.

Rebranding Means Connecting the Dots Differently

I rebranded myself though several career shifts, none more dramatic and traumatic than my first one. I started my professional life as a curatorial assistant in Japanese art at the Seattle Art Museum. Then I went on to work on a PhD at Harvard, even spending two years in Japan researching my dissertation and translating a Japanese art book into English. So my brand screamed "Japanese art historian."

Then, after eight years, I concluded that I was on the wrong path. So, I decided at the ripe age of twenty-eight to come to New York City and seek my fortune in branding and advertising, areas of interest I had explored as an undergraduate before settling on art history.

Initially, my credentials branded me as an "academic," and they were getting me nowhere, even with the Harvard brand. My negative interview experience changed only after I completely redid my résumé and rewrote my brand story—emphasizing the marketing, PR, event planning, and writing aspects of the job at the Seattle Art Museum and downplaying the academics. Mind you, everything was accurate, but the focus now was on the parts of my background that resonated with the brand I was aspiring to be. You don't have to include everything you've ever done on your résumé, but you need to be honest and accurate as you gear it toward your new goals.

With my revised résumé and elevator speech, I positioned myself as a "marketer of difficult products" and compared successfully marketing Asian art shows in the West to marketing difficult products. My pitch clicked and I got my start in branding and advertising.

When You Really Need to Rebrand

The key to rebranding is doing things that counter the unfair typecasting you've been given so that people begin to see you differently. A dramatic example is Hillary Clinton. As First Lady she was criticized for overstepping—for attending Cabinet meetings, for attempting to put together a health-care plan, and other perceived transgressions. America wasn't ready for an activist First Lady, and her public perception hurt her popularity in polls at the time. But by the time she became secretary of state, she was one of the most admired people in the world.

So what did she do to bring about this monumental turnaround? Clinton began her transformation shortly after leaving the White House, when she decided to run for U.S. senator in New York State. She started from scratch and went on "listening tours" around the state. She did her homework and impressed locals by listening to their concerns and by her knowledge of their region. Once elected, she didn't play the diva as a celebrity senator hogging the cameras. She kept a low profile crafting legislation behind the scenes. Later, as secretary of state, she kept on going with her diplomatic agenda no mater what storms were brewing domestically. People began to see Hillary Clinton differently and to admire her abilities.

Another time to rebrand is when you're caught in a scandal, particularly if it spills into the media. Although a scandal of these proportions is not likely to happen to you (or me), strong female brands have survived even mega body blows by doing things that counter negative perceptions.

Martha Stewart was convicted of insider trading and did time behind bars, but she began her comeback the minute she left prison wearing a gray poncho hand-made by a fellow inmate. The poncho telegraphed important messages: she bonded with a fellow inmate, she was transformed by this experience, and she was back in control of her brand.

Most of us don't need to rebrand because we've been exposed in a highly publicized scandal; we are more likely to rebrand when we're stuck or we've lost our job, like my client "Leah." A successful business development professional at a large technology company, Leah found herself marginalized when a new boss came in who favored salespeople with a technical background. Six months later she got a poor performance review. Then she was downsized as part of a major corporate restructuring.

Unlike when she started out, now the job opportunities were in more innovative technologies and in social media, where she had some (although limited) experience. To fill in the gaps she took online courses and attended workshops in emerging technologies and social media. In her résumé and LinkedIn profile, Leah rebranded herself as a "senior business development executive who leverages sales through social media" and emphasized those aspects of her background and recent credentials. The rebranding worked when Leah took her new brand to market with an online campaign on social media and an offline campaign of phone calls, emails, letters, and interviews.

If You Don't Market Yourself, Who Will?

A complaint that I hear from many professional women is that they were part of successful projects in the past but they didn't save anything so they don't have any tangible or digital materials to market their success stories. Don't let that be you. As a Woman Who Brands, you need to collect *marketing materials* and put together a *brag book*, with paper and digital records of your success stories and accomplishments. You can put these items on your website or link to them on your LinkedIn profile where appropriate, or have them in a folder or portfolio for interviews. Here are the kinds of marketing materials you should be gathering:

- **Recommendation letters and notes of recognition:** In addition to formal recommendation or testimonial letters, save e-mails from bosses, clients, and colleagues complimenting you on a project well done.

- **Awards of achievement:** If there is a formal awards ceremony at your company, have a colleague take a picture of you receiving the award.
- **Samples and marketing materials of key projects:** Try to collect both digital and actual reports, brochures, and the like.
- **Metrics that convey proof of performance:** Keep spreadsheets and reports that show the metrics on how well a project was executed.
- **Key initiatives and achievements in a case study format:** Have a nicely formatted document that shows challenge, action, and results as if it were a new business pitch.
- **Pictures and videos of you in professional situations:** If you speak or are part of a panel at a business conference, be sure to have it recorded with photos or a video, and save your slides.
- **Web screen shots:** Take screen shots of company or professional websites where you appear so you have a record of your business activities.

You Can Say It's Luck

The most important thing you can do if you want your career to break out is to be an ambassador for Brand You. Get out of your department. Meet people in other areas. Volunteer for unexpected projects. Show interest in the work outside of your area. Learn the subtle art of self-promotion both in person and online.

You have to take responsibility for your career. Behind any successful product, politician, celebrity, business executive, or cause is smart branding. People may attribute their extraordinary success to hard work or good fortune, but if you examine the careers of successful people in a range of arenas, you'll find creative, strategic branding every step of the way. Maybe there was some "luck" along the way, but most likely they created the luck by putting themselves in auspicious situations, like getting their work in front of people who matter or volunteering for a committee at their industry association to meet new people.

But that doesn't mean that you can't attribute your career success to luck. Many women at the top attribute success to luck or say it "just happened," like Marissa Mayer, CEO of Yahoo. But a careful study of successful people—men and women—suggest otherwise.

Luck is the little white lie behind many people's success stories because it's more appealing to people than telling the truth. Namely, that you've been working 24/7 on your career. Luck makes people look like they didn't plan their success or consciously promote themselves to people who count. And luck is a helpful element for women to include in their career story since in most cultures being an *ambitious* woman is not a compliment.

So leave a role for Lady Luck but realize that almost no one achieves great things or becomes a well-known self-brand without wanting it, working hard to achieve it, and mastering personal branding. Strategy, creativity, and reaching out have more to do with achieving success than luck does.

So if you say, "Gee, I just got lucky. The CEO was looking for someone to head up the new global initiative and I guess I was in the right place at the right time," or "I didn't plan for this to happen," people will respond in a positive way. But in reality, recognize that the real formula for success includes smart branding.

Take Charge of Your Most Important Asset

One of the most positive developments for the world's future is the celebration of female leadership. No woman has done more in recent years to put women's leadership foremost in the world's consciousness than Facebook COO Sheryl Sandberg and her book, *Lean In*. The book has been a best-seller and sparked a vibrant, much-needed conversation about women, leadership, and the way women can curtail their own career success.

Sandberg's book and her TED talk were brilliant personal branding for her, too, since they gave her high visibility and a platform, women's leadership, that no other high-level businesswomen were addressing as boldly as she did. No longer just a top business executive, Sandberg is a business celebrity, likely the most famous female business executive in the world today. Her brand is about something bigger and more meaningful than mere business—it's about transforming the world through a more equal, gender-diverse workplace.

With our collaborative, inclusive leadership style, women are leading in a way that doesn't seek to have power over people as much as to empower people. Women are opening up the forum for broader communication and problem solving in the professional world, a distinct advantage in today's competitive, global workplace. We have an uncanny empathy and intuition that helps us read a room or situation, or gauge how we're coming across. Many women aren't afraid to put caring and warmth into the professional equation to create a personal feeling as a leader. After all, it's in our DNA to cultivate connection and relationships. Many of us use our verbal agility to shine in communicating at work and our edge in visual identity to bring color and style to the workplace.

Follow the lead of women who brand. Don't fall into the trap of thinking, "I'm not ready," and be open to taking career risks. Make a commitment to own your value and your accomplishments and learn how to be your best advocate. It won't be a straight trajectory to the top. It never is. But with a personal branding mindset, you won't give up—you'll retool and relaunch Brand You.

Branding gives you a process for maximizing these female-based assets and the unique asset that is you. Personal branding is closely linked to the desire for personal improvement, growth, and achieving goals. It gives you the tools to fill in the missing pieces of the puzzle so that others will have positive impressions about Brand You, and you will too.

At every point in your professional life, there are different options and opportunities. But if you're true to yourself and take charge of your brand, you'll find the right strategy and tactics to withstand any storm and address the big issues in your life.

As Mom said, "It's up to you."

THERE'S NO RECIPE FOR SUCCESS OR STYLE

Elizabeth Hitchcock

director of strategy and innovation, AT&T

I'm a survivor. My parents divorced when I was a teenager and suddenly I found myself on my own, more or less, to apply to colleges, seek scholarships, and launch my own career. That early hardship of being caught up in the trauma of a messy divorce was, in a way, a good thing because it made me determined. Throw me your must-do, most difficult project and I will figure it out.

I've had the privilege of working in business development at technology start-ups and some of the top innovation-based brands in the world. And now I'm the social media strategist at a major global telecommunications company. But the most rewarding and exciting thing I do is mentor other women. Young, and even middle-aged, women come to me for advice on careers and many of them tell me that my mentorship has helped transform their lives. Well, I've been transformed, too, from a private career woman who did my own thing, to a very visible person actively involved with social media like Twitter, my blog "intrepidsocialgal," and hands-on involvement in various women's organizations.

I never planned to be a mentor to women. It simply happened. Then, because I've been interested in clothes and in the dynamics on how to present yourself, many women started to ask me about personal appearance in addition to the career advice. There's no real recipe for putting together your own style. You have to have courage and a sense of yourself. It takes time. You need to go about it thoughtfully. It's not just what you wear, it's who you are. Developing your own style can be a painful process of self-discovery. Women often thank me for giving them the courage to be themselves. One even told me, "My God, if I don't have to look like every else, maybe I don't have to think like everyone else, either"

Like it or not, in our society, people judge you by your clothes, your hair, your style, and the labels you wear, or how you put it all together. Here are some thoughts on creating your personal style:

Dressing should be fun. I consider myself a sponge. You have to have an open mind and an open eye. I never start out with a specific purchase in mind, for me it's the thrill of the hunt. I buy things that are appropriate for my work, flattering to my body, and, most of all, feel like me.

Mix it up. I can buy things from anywhere and everywhere. I enjoy putting things together so I might mix a couture piece with something I got at J. Crew or Target. I don't care where things come from. Even when I buy a designer suit, I'll buy something out of character for the designer and change the belt or something to make it mine.

Start with something simple and well cut. I start with: a dress or top and skirt that are very simple, very well cut with strong lines and structure. But for you, your look may be more flowing things. That's what you need to discover.

Choose accessories that jump out. Find unusual, interesting accessories and jewelry that convey your style and finish off the look.

Use color to give punch to your look. I never met a color I didn't like. There's some tone of every color that can work. Don't limit yourself to the color the fashion magazines are promoting for the season. Have the courage to define your own brand colors.

To be attractive you must look real. You need to look relaxed and not uptight in the way you dress. Wearing Jimmy Choo's and Manolo's with six-inch heels and two straps can make sense for the evening but my secret for business settings is platform shoes that give me height but don't make walking a balancing act.

Tip your hat to style. I'm interested in style, but I interpret style so that it fits me, my career and lifestyle. Don't be brainwashed by the fashion press. You decide, not the media.

Don't neglect your hair or adding a personal touch. I used to have bad hair days until I discovered hair extensions, pop-on ponytails, and hair wraps or buns. They're a great workaround when your hair isn't behaving. If your hair looks good and you have an outfit that looks good on you, you're 80 percent there. Have fun with the other 20 percent and make it Brand You.

ACKNOWLEDGMENTS

Female intuition gave me the idea to write this book, but acting on it took the inspiration, stories, suggestions, and support of hundreds of people.

First, my special thanks to Gary Andrew Gulkis, my book collaborator, who provided the poet's gift for language to know the right word and to help me try to craft the text with style and elegance. As a representative of that other gender, he provided invaluable balance, insight, and humor and helped to keep me challenged and focused on the larger truth. This book became dramatically better through his generous participation.

In developing this book, I interviewed well over one hundred women, successful women one and all—women in their twenties, thirties, forties, fifties, sixties, and seventies. What a treasure trove of insights and passion about women and success. Thanks especially to Elizabeth Hitchcock, who shared her story and was exceptionally generous with her support for this project. Thanks to all the women who let me use their stories and point of view in my book: Meenu Chhabra, Deborah Elam, Paula Forman, Kirsten Gillibrand, Joi Gordon, Rosalind Hudnell, Fiona Hutchinson, Graciela Meibar, Pam Paton, Barbara Res, Marcia Roosevelt, Carol Ross, Edwina Sandys, Muriel Siebert, Gena Testar, Billie Ida Williamson, and Melinda Wolfe. I want to thank professors Alice Eagly, Roy Baumeister, and David Klappholz for their insight.

The list of people I interviewed is too long to detail here, but I especially want to thank the following for their suggestions, stories and thoughts on the female brand: Sylvia Acevedo, Yoshiko Aiba, Jean Andersen, Iris Apfel, Nomi Bachar, Roy Baumeister, Aishwarya Bhat, Tom Blanco, Kevin Renee Bishop, Nora Brennan, Carolyn Buck Luce, Georgina Carnegie, Arlene Castrovinci, Jodi Charles, Sue Chiafullo, Karen Christensen, Kathy Connelly, Paul Copcutt, Tim Davis, Kathie DeChirico, Eli Dickson Vicki Donlon, Theresa M. Ellis, Anne Erni, Susan Esper, Tiffany Esposito, Dr. Vincent Esposito, Sandy Evans, Joe and Veronica Fabio, Joan Ford, Barbara Glasser, Sherry Glazer, Maria

Gotsch, Susan Jacobs, Jeannie Kahwajy, Mary Kapka, Karen Kesner, Beth-Ellen Keyes, Jill Klein, Barbara Krafte, Pamela Larrick, Starlin Leitner, Roberta Maguire, Terry Mamendo, Pauline Mohr, Faith Monson, Diane Morgan, Elizabeth Nieto, Ginny O'Brien, Young-Mi Park, Vasso Petrou, Marcia Roosevelt, Nancy Rutter, Eileen Smith, Beverly Tarulli, Sherri Smith, Lisa Watts, Denise Sena and Margaret Yelland. Many thanks to Polina Viro for her technical skills in marketing the book online and redesigning my website.

Writing a book can be an arduous ordeal. That's why having a great publishing team is so critical, and my team at Nicholas Brealey actually made it fun. At the top of my list to thank is Nick Brealey, who has now supported me through three books. Thanks, Nick. Jennifer Delaney put her publishing, production, and editing muscle behind this project, for which I am grateful. A special thanks to Chuck Dresner, who has led the sales effort for all my books with care and his personal touch. Thanks to the other members of the Nicholas Brealey team: Jennifer Campaniolo, Janet Crockett, and Nadia Manuelli for making the marketing and publishing process run so smoothly. Thanks also to Susan Lauzau for copyediting the book so skillfully, as she has my last two books.

I want to thank my Sisterhood of Supporters, my three sisters Kevin, Jean, and Joan, and our mother, who gave me the inspiration and drive to write this book and who gave all four of her daughters the desire and determination to have a career along with whatever else we might want to do with our lives. Thanks, Mom!

ABOUT THE AUTHOR

Catherine Kaputa
president, SelfBrand www.selfbrand.com
brand strategist, speaker, and author

From Madison Avenue to Wall Street to the halls of academe, Catherine Kaputa perfected her ability to market products, places, and companies. She learned brand strategy from marketing gurus Al Ries and Jack Trout, and then led the award-winning "I ♥ NY" campaign at Wells, Rich, Greene. For over ten years she was SVP, director of advertising and community affairs at Citi Smith Barney, and she taught branding at New York University's Stern School of Business.

Yet Catherine discovered that one of the most important applications for branding is not for products or companies—it's for individuals to define and own their career identity and create their own performance success. That's why Catherine launched SelfBrand LLC, a New York City-based personal branding company, and started speaking to groups and coaching executives, employees, and entrepreneurs on personal branding.

A High-Energy Speaker

Catherine Kaputa cut her teeth in branding in three of the most demanding and innovative environments: Madison Avenue, Wall Street, and a top-five business school. Now, Catherine shares those experiences with others.

Catherine Kaputa is known for her compelling content and entertaining style, using storytelling, branding insight, and humor in a keynote tailored for each audience. Her topics are:

- **Personal Branding: Brand Yourself for Success**, based on ideas in her award-winning book, *You Are a Brand: In Person and Online, How Smart People Brand Themselves for Success*

- **Women's Leadership: Creating More Female Leaders**, based on ideas in *Women Who Brand: How Smart Women Promote Themselves and Get Ahead*
- **Entrepreneurship and Product Branding: Brand Your Business/Brand You**, based on the ideas in her award-winning book, *Breakthrough Branding: How Entrepreneurs and Intrapreneurs Transform a Small Idea into a Big Brand*

In addition to keynote presentations, Catherine also does half-day and full-day seminars on branding. Often, companies bring her in when launching a women's initiative or a professional development program, or during times of transition. For sales professionals, she does talks and workshops on virtual branding and social selling as ways to grow business revenues, attract new clients, and nurture existing clients. Companies also bring her in when introducing a new marketing program consistent with the concepts in *Breakthrough Branding*. Using vivid case studies and branding principles, her presentations provide branding support for the company's new program with employees, media, and investors.

An Award-Winning Author

Catherine wrote the definitive book on personal branding, *You Are a Brand!*, winner of the Ben Franklin Award for Best Career Book, a bronze IPPY Award, and a Top Ten Business Training Book in China. It has been translated over 10 languages and is now out in an expanded and updated second edition: www.youareabrandbook.com

Catherine's book, *Breakthrough Branding*, on innovation, branding, and creativity, won the Silver Medal in *Foreword* magazine's 2012 Book of the Year Awards, Business/Economics category: www.breakthroughbrandingbook.com

Catherine's other great passion is women's leadership and creating more female leaders, the topic of *Women Who Brand*, an expanded and updated paperback version of her hardcover book, *The Female Brand*.

Catherine has been featured on CNN, ABC, NBC, MSNBC, *The Wall Street Journal*, *The New York Times*, *USA Today*, *The Financial Times*, *Fortune*, *Harvard Business Review Online*, *Fast Company*, *Wired*, and other media. Catherine has a B.A. from Northwestern University and was a Ph.D. candidate at Harvard University.

Corporate Sales

Catherine's books are an excellent merchandising gift for customers, employees or clients:

Women Who Brand for high-potential women employees and female clients who want empower themselves and their companies to create more female leaders

You Are a Brand! for anyone—customers, employees, executives—who wants to learn how to apply the principles and strategies from the commercial world of brands to your most important product, Brand You.

Breakthrough Branding for entrepreneurs and innovation-based companies where everyone needs to be a growth agent and know how to transform ideas into brands.

For quantity discount pricing or customization, please contact the book's publisher, Nicholas Brealey Publishing, sales-us@nicholas-brealey.com or call 617-523-3801. For international rights, contact: rights@nicholasbrealey.com.

For information about Catherine Kaputa and her keynote talks, visit her website, www.selfbrand.com; her branding blog, www.artofbranding .com; her women's leadership blog, www.womenwhobrand.com, or contact Catherine@selfbrand.com.

NOTES

Introduction

A comprehensive discussion of the research around female leadership can be found in Sheryl Sandberg's trend-setting book, *Lean In* (New York: Alfred A. Knopf, 2013).

The study of prepubescent boys and girls discussed by Professor Donelson Forsyth was broadcast in *The Infinite Mind*, on National Public Radio. See "The Infinite Mind: Groups" at www.infinitemind.org or www.lemedia.com/mind9929.htm. An Israeli study with pre-schoolers showed that boys are fifty times more likely than girls to use competition and physical means, while girls use talking and taking turns. Susan Pinker, *The Sexual Paradox: Men, Women and the Real Gender Gap* (New York: Scribner, 2008), 199–200.

The fact that women are twice as likely as men to suffer from depression has been widely documented; see "New Report on Women and Depression: Latest Research Findings and Recommendations," American Psychological Association, www.apa.org/releases/depression report.html. More than 90 percent of people with eating disorders are women; see www.4woman.gov/owh/pub/factsheets/eatingdis.htm. For information on male aggression, violence, and alcohol abuse, see *Alcohol Alert*, National Institute on Alcohol Abuse and Alcoholism, no. 38 (October 1997), http://pubs.niaaa.nih.gov/publications/aa38.htm.

Citing the research of Herbert Marsh and others, Malcolm Gladwell talks extensively about the importance of feeling smart relative to your peers in the context of the "Big Fish–Little Pond Effect" (BFLPE) and the concept of "relative deprivation" in his book *David and Goliath* (New York: Little Brown and Company, 2013), chapter 3. For the research behind the BFLPE, see Marjorie Seaton, et.al. "Big-Fish-Little-Pond Effect: Generalizability and Moderation—Two Sides of the Same Coin," http://isites.harvard.edu/fs/docs/icb.topic741392.files/BigFish.pdf.

The research on gender differences is extensive. In discussing brain differences and female-male aptitudes throughout the book I was very indebted to the work of Simon Baron-Cohen, *The Essential Difference: The Truth about the Male and Female Brain* (New York: Basic Books, 2003). See also Louann Brizendene, *The Female Brain* (New York:

Random House, 2007) and Susan Pinker, *The Sexual Paradox: Men, Women and the Real Gender Gap* (New York: Scribner, 2008).

Read Roy F. Baumeister's delightful talk, "Is There Anything Good About Men?" an address to the American Psychological Association, 2007, available on the web. I am also indebted to Professor Baumeister for sharing his views with me over the phone on male-female differences and a range of gender topics. See also, Roy F. Baumeister and Kristin L. Sommer, "What Do Men Want? Gender Differences and Two Spheres of Belongingness: comment on Cross and Madson (1997)," *Psychological Bulletin*, 1997, Vol. 122, No. 1, 38–44.

See Daniel Goleman, *Social Intelligence: The New Science of Human Relationships* (New York: Bantam, 2007) for an in-depth discussion of the new findings in neuroscience.

For a discussion of gender and STEM careers, see Diane F. Halpern, Camilla P. Benbow, David C. Geary, Ruben C Gur, Janet Shibley Hyde, and Morton Anne Gernsbacher, "Sex, Math and Scientific Achievement," *Scientific American*, November 28, 2007. For the Study of Mathematically Precocious Youth (SMPY), see https://my.vanderbilt.edu/smpy/

Chapter I

The women's research organization, Catalyst, has done a number of research studies on barriers to women's success, see "Sponsoring Women to Success," Catalyst, 2011, http://www.catalyst.org/knowledge/sponsoring-women-success; "Damned If You Do, Doomed If You Don't," Catalyst, 2107, http://www.catalyst.org/knowledge/double-bind-dilemma-women-leadership-damned-if-you-do-doomed-if-you-dont-0.

The research on "Male Hubris/Female Humility Effect" was done by Professor Adrian Furnham, of University College London, who examined thirty studies of sex differences in IQ and found that women on average predict their IQ score five points lower than men do, see http://www.ucl.ac.uk/news/news-articles/0904/09042001. Women's tendencies to downplay achievements and not self-promote is supported by a number of research studies.

Simon Baron-Cohen, *The Essential Difference: The Truth about the Male and Female Brain* (New York: Basic Books, 2003). Baron-Cohen has done extensive research on gender differences in children including day old infants as well as adults.

For a discussion of the branding of "The South Beach Diet," see Jeffrey A. Trachtenberg's article, "Diet Book Found Novel Ways to Get to

Top—and Stay, *The Wall Street Journal*, June 30, 2004, http://online
wsj.com/news/articles/SB108855292365851094.

Chapter 3

For a good overall discussion of likeability, see Tim Sanders, *The Like-
ability Factor* (New York: Three Rivers Press, 2006). Also see "Women
Like Women More Than Men Like Men, According to Study," *Science
Daily*, December 22, 2004, and the *Journal of Personality and Social
Psychology*, October, 2004, for an account of the research done by Pur-
due's Women Studies Program.

The Q Score was developed in 1963 by Marketing Evaluations, Inc., a
United States company based in Manhasset, New York, to measure the
familiarity and appeal of a brand, company, celebrity, cartoon character, or television show.

Daniel Goleman has done a considerable body of work on emotional
intelligence and social intelligence, see his books, *Emotional Intelligence: Why It Can Matter More Than IQ* (New York: Bantam, 2005),
and *Emotional Intelligence, Social Intelligence: The New Science of
Human Relationships* (New York: Bantam, 2007). For a discussion of
intuition and gut feelings, see also Gerd Gigerenzer, *Gut Feelings, The
Intelligence of the Unconscious* (New York: Viking, 2007).

Chapter 4

The classic book on gender differences in communication is Deborah
Tannen's *You Just Don't Understand: Women and Men in Conversation* (New York: William Morrow & Co, 1990).

Malcolm Gladwell brought the term "mitigated speech" into the national
consciousness in his book *Outliers*. In the book, he talked about the
phenomenon in terms of air crashes in which a co-pilot or other junior
member of the flight team is afraid to speak up because it could be
disrespectful toward the pilot. So they use indirect talk to soften the
meaning of what they are trying to say, sometimes resulting in disaster.
Today, flight crews are coached on the problems of mitigated language.
The 6 Degrees of Mitigation cited are adapted from Ute Fischer and
Judith Orasanu, "Cultural Diversity and Crew Communication," paper
presented at Astronautical Congress, Amsterdam; American Institute
of Aeronautics and Astronautics (1999).

Marshall Goldsmith writes about the communication style of successful CEOs and executives. See Marshall Goldsmith, *What Got You Here
Won't Get You There* (New York: Hyperion, 2007).

UCLA professor Albert Mehrabian has done pioneering work on the importance of verbal and nonverbal messages. For an overview of his work, see http://en.wikipedia.org/wiki/Albert_Mehrabian.

Daniel Goleman has written about the emotional wasteland of e-mail communication; see "E-Mail Is Easy to Write (and to Misread)," *The New York Times*, October 7, 2007.

Chapter 5

There have been a number of studies and articles on the different way women and men use social media. See Helen Nowicka, "Men Are from Foursquare, Women Are from Facebook," Porter Novelli, February, 2012; "Women on the Web: How Women Are Shaping the Internet," ComScore, 2012; Albert Sun, et.al., "A Week on Foursquare: Where Do Men and Women Go?" *The Wall Street Journal*, May 19, 2011.

Chapter 6

There have been multiple studies and articles on the "beauty premium." The mock labor market study called "Why Beauty Matters" was conducted by Markus Mobius of the Harvard economics department and Tanya Rosenblat of Wesleyan University. You can read the abstract on the web at http://trosenblat.web.wesleyan.edu/home/beauty2005.pdf.

A British and Italian team did the longitudinal study on the beauty premium using decades of data on more than 8,000 men and women who left school in Wisconsin in 1957; see Emanuela Sala, et. al., "Exploring the Impact of Male and Female Facial Attractiveness on Occupational Prestige," published in *Research in Social Stratification and Mobility*, Volume 31, March 2013, 69–81.

For the research studies showing that the medial orbitofrontal cortex of the brain is involved in rating both the beauty of a face and the goodness of a behavior, see Takashi Tsukiura and Roberto Cabeza, "Remembering Beauty: Roles of Orbitofrontal and Hippocampal Regions in Successful Memory Encoding of Attractive Faces," *Neuro-Image*, Volume 54, Issue 1, 1 January 2011, 653–660. I also relied on a discussion of their work by Robert M. Sapolsky, "Pretty Smart? Why We Equate Beauty with Truth," *Wall Street Journal*, January 17, 2014.

For research done on attractive CEOs and stock price, see the paper by two University of Wisconson professors, Joseph T. Halford and Scott H.C. Hsu, "Beauty Is Wealth: CEO Appearance and Shareholder Value," http://papers.ssrn.com/sol3/papers.cfm?abstract_id=2357756.

The economist Daniel Hamermesh has been studying the financial benefits of looks for over two decades. Hamermesh calculates that the typical worker gets a "beauty premium" of up to $230,000 over the course of a career. See *Beauty Pays: Why Attractive People Are More Successful* (Princeton, NJ: Princeton University Press, 2013). For additional studies on how attractiveness is perceived and rewarded in the workplace, see Dr. Daniel Hamermesh and Jeff E. Biddle, "Beauty and the Labor Market," http://ideas.repec.org/p/nbr/nberwo/4518.html.

For the attractiveness principle at work with babies, see Robert Lee Hotz, "Some Scientists Argue We Are Built to Coo at the Sight of a Baby," *The Wall Street Journal*, April 4, 2008. For attractiveness on the job, see Sue Shellenbarger, "On the Job, Beauty Is More Than Skin-Deep," *Wall Street Journal*, October 27, 2011.

Malcolm Gladwell's popular book *Blink, The Power of Thinking Without Thinking* (New York: Back Bay Books, 2007) is about the power of thin slicing and first impressions. New York University has done research on microthinslicing, including one study that found that people make eleven decisions about others in the first seven seconds.

A team at Harvard Business School led by Amy Cuddy has done a series of studies on power poses, see Cuddy's TED talk, "Your Body Language Shapes Who You Are," which has been seen by more than 10 million viewers, http://www.ted.com/talks/amy_cuddy_your_body_language_shapes_who_you_are.html; Amy J. C. Cuddy, et. al., "The Benefit of Power Posing Before a High-Stakes Social Evaluation," *Harvard Business School Working Paper*, No. 13-027, September 2012. http://dash.harvard.edu/handle/1/9547823.

Chapter 7

For a comprehensive study on the female leadership style, see Alice H. Eagly and Linda L. Carli, *Through the Labyrinth*; Alice H. Eagly and M. C. Johannesen-Schmict, "Transformational, Transactional, and Laissez-Faire Leadership Styles: A Meta-Analysis Comparing Women and Men," *Journal of Social Issues*, 57, 781–797. I also want to thank Professor Eagly for her thoughtful responses to my e-mails.

There are numerous books and articles on the Myers-Briggs assessment test and gender differences. See also www.myersbriggs.org.

For research on the workaholic tendencies of male CEOs, see Roy F. Baumeister's talk, "Is There Anything Good About Men?" an address to the American Psychological Association, 2007, available on the web.

For an accounting of Abraham Lincoln and his team of rivals, see Doris Kearns Goodwin, *Team of Rivals: The Political Genius of Abraham Lincoln* (New York: Simon & Schuster, 2005), 99–100.

Chapter 9

For studies on the influential nature of others taste in music, see Kurt Kiener, "Your Taste in Music Is Shaped by the Crowd," *New Scientist*, February 9, 2006.

Chapter 10

For a discussion of the Harvard Business School women's problem, see Jodi Kantor, "Harvard Business School Case Study," *New York Times*, September 7, 2013, http://www.nytimes.com/2013/09/08/education/harvard-case-study-gender-equity.html?_r=0.

Soraya Roberts, "Are Women as Competitive as Men?" *The Daily Beast*, December 11, 2013, http://www.thedailybeast.com/witw/articles/2013/12/11/female-competition-it-s-not-just-about-men.html.

Malcolm Gladwell discusses "relative deprivation" and "Big Fish–Little Pond" in chapter 3 of *David and Goliath* (New York: Little Brown & Company, 2013).

For a discussion of power poses, see Amy Cuddy, "Your Body Language Shapes Who You Are," TED talk, http://www.ted.com/talks/amy_cuddy_your_body_language_shapes_who_you_are.html, Amy J. C. Cuddy, et. al., "The Benefit of Power Posing Before a High-Stakes Social Evaluation," *Harvard Business School Working Paper*, No. 13-027, September 2012. http://dash.harvard.edu/handle/1/9547823.

Barbara Corcoran has talked about her career success in various media, see "How to Steal the Market from Your Competitor," *LinkedIn*, November 5, 2013, and her delightful books: Barbara Corcoran and Bruce Littlefield, *Shark Tales: How I Turned $1,000 into a Billion Dollar Business* (New York: Portfolio, 2011), and Barbara Corcoran and Bruce Littlefield, *Use What You've Got, and Other Business Lessons I Learned From My Mom* (New York: Portfolio, 2003).

For an introduction to the "Imposter Syndrome," see Pauline Rose Clance and Suzanne Imes, "The Imposter Phenomenon in High Achieving Women: Dynamics and Therapeutic Intervention," http://www.paulineroseclance.com/pdf/ip_high_achieving_women.pdf.

For a fascinating discussion of Marissa Mayer and her leadership style, see Bethany McLean, "Yahoo's Geek Goddess," *Vanity Fair*,

January 2014, http://www.vanityfair.com/business/2014/01/marissa-mayer-yahoo-google.

For an interesting discussion of Angela Merkel's career, see Frank Jordans, "Angela Merkel's Rise to Power: How German's First Female Chancellor Achieved Historic Success," http://www.huffingtonpost.com/2013/09/19/angela-merkel-first-female-chancellor_n_3954002.html.

Dilma Rousseff's makeover has been discussed in multiple sources, for English, see Ana Clara Costa, "Dilma Rousseff Gets an Extreme Makeover," http://www.huffingtonpost.com/ana-clara-costa/dilma-rousseff-style-photos_b_802187.html#s214263title=April_2004.

For a comprehensive discussion of the confidence gap between men and women, read, Katty Kay and Claire Shipmen, *The Confidence Coed: The Science and Art of Self Assurance—What Women should Know* (NY: Harper Business 2014).

INDEX